MW01520428

A WALK WITHIN

JACQUELINE COMPAGNONI

Halo ●●●●
Publishing International

ISBN 13: 978-1-61244-314-0
Library of Congress Control Number: 2014918586

Printed in the United States of America

Published by Halo Publishing International
1100 NW Loop 410
Suite 700 - 176
San Antonio, Texas 78213
Toll Free 1-877-705-9647
www.halopublishing.com
www.holapublishing.com
e-mail: contact@halopublishing.com

In memory of Debbie Compagnoni. You left your fingerprints of compassion and selflessness on our lives. You will always be loved and missed.

To my father, Louie, thank you for caring for and providing for our family, even in the difficult times. Thank you for always lending a listening ear and being there when I need you.

To my sister, Christina, you are an amazing, loving sister and friend. I can never thank you enough for sticking by my side throughout all my bad choices. Thank you for being an inspirational mother to your children.

To my brother, David, your tender heart and giving spirit is a blessing. Thank you for all that you do for our family and for being an inspirational father to your children. Thank you for always being there to help me in my many times of need.

To all the young ladies in my life, you are truly Warrior Princesses.

To all of those that have helped me along my journey, stood by my side and never gave up on me, thank you!

Table of Contents

"YOU ARE UGLY. YOU ARE WORTHLESS. YOU ARE STUPID. NO ONE WILL EVER LOVE YOU. YOU ARE GOING TO FAIL. JUST GIVE UP. JUST GIVE IN. YOU AREN'T GOING TO AMOUNT TO ANYTHING."

Those are the words I grew up hearing. What I later realized was that there was a quiet voice whispering to me: "You are beautiful. You are special. You are smart. You can move mountains. I have a plan for you."

My story starts at a very young age. I grew up in Chicago in a neighborhood where, when a car backfires, everyone ducks for cover. My childhood home was a shabby little apartment building where you could hear the fighting and screaming from the neighbors through the walls as you were trying to sleep. My mother was easily angered and quick to yell. My father was full of rage and would beat my mother, my siblings, and myself. This is what I remember about my childhood. I grew up hearing my parents fight and scream at each other, until one day my father left. I was only nine years old when he left. This forced my mother to raise three children on her own. It wasn't long before she began to medicate herself with alcohol.

Prologue

Eighteen-year-old Marianna had started her day like all the others. She woke up early, got dressed, and headed off to the diner to wait tables. It was during the lunch rush hour when he walked in. His dark black, silky hair and baby blue eyes caught her attention from across the room. She noticed his dark blue security uniform and wished for a moment that she could have the feeling of security in her life. She wished she had someone to protect her from all the monsters in the world.

Roger gave her a warm smile as she approached him. She greeted him as she did so many other customers that morning and got him settled at a table. The conversation between them remained quite simple as the lunch rush kept hold of Marianna's attention. Before Roger slipped away to head back to work, he quickly jotted down his name and number on a napkin and handed it to Marianna. Marianna turned a deep shade of red, smiled, and agreed to give him a call. After Roger left, Marianna found herself daydreaming. Throughout the rest of her shift, she mixed up orders, lost focus, dropped a glass, and ran over several of her coworkers. She was so absorbed in the brief moment she had with Roger. Could he really be interested?

Marianna left work just after six. She clocked out and headed for the bus, reaching it just in time. On the ride home she recalled Roger's deep, masculine voice. She replayed the brief conversation they had and pulled out the napkin with his name and number on it. She gently stroked the edges as she stared at it. Roger, his name was Roger. That sounded like a nice name. *The name of a strong, protective man*, she thought. Marianna decided that she would call him when she got home.

Over the next few weeks, Marianna and Roger talked on the phone almost every night. When they were not working they spent time watching movies, talking, and getting to know each other. It didn't seem possible, but she felt so connected to Roger. He was everything she was looking for. The age difference didn't seem to bother Roger, so Marianna decided that it wouldn't bother her either. It's not like he was much older, only six years. Besides, she was looking for someone mature to care for her.

It was about five months into their relationship when Marianna found out that she was pregnant. She was not sure what to do. She didn't want to lose Roger. In the end, she decided that she needed to tell him and hoped that he would not leave her, like her father had abandoned her mother. Roger didn't leave her. To Marianna's surprise, he actually asked her to marry him.

A trip to the Justice of the Peace and they were officially married. Two months later, Susan was born. Marianna and Roger had moved into a small, barely affordable apartment. When possible, Roger picked up overtime and Marianna returned to work at the diner. The cost of daycare took a toll on their budget and required both of them to work long hours.

Susan was eager to learn and try things on her own. As a baby she would curiously watch everything in her surroundings, taking it all in. As a toddler she was eager to learn to walk. No matter how many times she fell down, she would keep at it until one day she just got up and toddled around.

When Roger couldn't be home to join her and Susan, Marianna would set dinner aside for him. Roger and Marianna spent the time they had together learning to care for little Susan.

A WALK WITHIN

Watching her as she learned how to do things on her own. When Susan was four years old, Amber was born. Amber was the complete opposite of Susan. Amber was quiet, cautious, and reserved. Susan was the big sister by all definitions. She was the protector and watched out for her baby sister. With the extra cost of another child, Roger had to pick up a second job. Marianna continued to wait tables and picked up extra shifts when possible. The finances were tight, but the family made do. Two years later, along came Jonathan. Jonathan was a ball of energy. He was always running around, knocking things over, and pestering his sisters.

Three children to take care of; the last thing that the Beckman family needed was to lose any source of income, let alone two. One afternoon, Marianna received an alarming call. Roger had slipped on some ice when leaving work and broke his back. It was a long road to recovery, and with the loss of both of Roger's incomes, bills went unpaid, stress increased, and the family had to apply for government assistance just to get by. And just like that, the honeymoon was over.

Chapter One: The Final Fight

CRASH! The breaking of glass startled me awake.

"Just get out of here!" I heard Mom scream.

"I don't know why I even bother!" Dad yelled back at her.

I buried my head under the pillows to drown out yet another screaming battle. It felt like forever before I heard a door slam shut and my mom sobbing. I didn't know what to do. After several minutes, I managed to get some courage and slowly walked toward the door. My legs went numb, I felt like my heart stopped beating, and I don't know how long it was before I started breathing again. When I cracked the door open, there was shattered glass all over the floor. Mom was at the kitchen table with her face buried in her hands. The floor creaked and I was no longer invisible.

"Susan, go to bed NOW!" Mom shouted from across the room.

I dared not question her or even give it another thought. I turned around, slammed the door, and stomped back toward the bed. My little brother and sister were staring up at me with puppy dog eyes, filled with tears. I was nine years old, the oldest of the three. My five-year-old sister, Amber, and Jonathan, the baby of the family, were both sitting on their beds with their legs tucked up close to their chest. Their looks told me what their words did not. They looked to me for protection. How could I protect them? I didn't know how to protect myself. The sounds of my siblings sobbing jolted me back to reality and I instantly went into my "motherly" routine.

"It's okay. Everything is fine," I said with a forced smile.

They both ran to me without hesitation. "Don't worry. Mommy and Daddy are just upset," I said, hoping that my voice didn't reveal my doubts.

Amber and Jonathan wrapped themselves around my body as to shield themselves from some unseen danger. I tucked them back in and sunk into my bed.

In the morning, Mom stood at the bedroom door yelling for us to get up and get ready for school. Jonathan was still too young to go to school, so during the day he went to stay with Lucy, our neighbor. I wiped the sleep from my eyes and hid in bed for another five minutes. It wasn't long after dozing back off that I heard Mom calling again. Dragging myself out of bed, I went over to wake up Amber and Jonathan. After a few shakes, they both got up and we all made our way to the kitchen. Mom put down three bowls and filled them with cereal. The kitchen was filled with a chilling silence. Mom was easily upset, so we knew better than to break the silence. Home was like a war zone, with us trying to avoid stepping on the land mines.

"Susan, get dressed. And help your brother and sister get dressed," my mother instructed, with a tone that told me not to dare fight her.

This was a morning routine. Mom didn't want to fuss with my brother and sister, so she had me do it. I escorted Jonathan and Amber to our room. Amber went to her drawer and picked an outfit to wear. I went with Jonathan to his drawer and picked out an outfit for him.

"NO! I DON'T WANT THAT ONE!" Jonathan yelled.

"Johnny…" That was my nickname for him. "This is the one you are going to wear," I told him with some nervousness in my voice. If Mom heard him having a fit, she might come in.

14

A WALK WITHIN

No one wanted that land mine to go off. "Johnny, just put this on. You don't want to upset Mommy." I gave him a look of warning.

However, Jonathan was still young and didn't understand. He continued ranting and went into a full tantrum. He began crying louder and before long, Mom entered the room.

"What is the problem?!" she came in yelling.

"Nothing, it's okay. He is just upset," I said, trying to keep control of the situation. "Come on Johnny, its okay".

However, it was too late. Mom's button was already pushed.

"Jonathan, how many times do I have to tell you? I need to get to work! *Stop it!* Jonathan, get back here!" Mom was now chasing Jonathan around the room.

When she got ahold of him, she wrestled him to the ground. She looked up at me with cold, angry eyes that bore deep into the pit of my stomach. "Give me his clothes," she ordered.

I gingerly made my way over to her with Jonathan's outfit, but before I could hand it over to her, she snatched them from my hands. Jonathan wiggled around on the floor, which ended with him kicking Mom in the face. That's all it took. WHAM! Mom smacked Jonathan across the face.

"Jonathan, stop kicking me! Forget it! You can go to Lucy's in your diaper for all I care!"

Mom stormed out of the room, leaving Jonathan wailing. I heard the front door slam shut and knew Mom left for work, once again leaving me to finish getting my siblings ready for the day. Once I dropped Jonathan off at Lucy's apartment, I needed to get Amber and myself on the school bus.

Amber and I sat there quietly during the ride. My thoughts lingered off into what the day ahead would be like. I supposed it would be just another day of Mrs. Fisher rambling on about history, science, or something or another. And Jillian…I don't know what I ever did to her. She was so mean. I wished there was someone I could talk to, but that would only make things worse. Then everyone would call me a tattletale.

It wasn't long before I was sitting in the classroom and the morning bell rang, signaling the start of the day. I found myself sitting, staring at the clock just above Mrs. Fisher's head. Time was moving so slowly. I couldn't focus on anything that she was going on and on about. Something didn't quite feel right. My mind began to wander.

Daddy and Mommy were arguing. Things were flying across the room. I was standing there just watching it all happen. How can I stop this? What can I do? I don't understand what is going on…

"All right class, close your books and line up in a single file at the door." Mrs. Fisher's voice jolted me back to reality. She had just finished her lesson, and lunchtime finally rolled around. I watched as the students around me did as instructed, and I followed suit.

Finally, 11:00 a.m. This day was taking forever. I had no idea what Mrs. Fisher was even teaching. *Oh, well,* I thought to myself.

Mrs. Fisher escorted our class to the cafeteria. My stomach was in knots. We reached our assigned tables and all sat down. I quickly glanced over my shoulder to see Jillian with her straight blond hair, blue eyes, and flirty smile. She threw her head back with a soft giggle. My stomach turned again, and I felt my cereal from breakfast churning in my stomach. Jillian Peterson got up with her table, twirling a strand of her golden blond hair. As she passed by me she threw me a glare that warned me not to dare even breathe in her direction. My neck became tense; the color from my hands and face drained, and the girl next to me asked if I was okay.

"I'm fine," I quickly lied.

Our table was called next and I pushed my seat back to get up. However, I never could have imagined causing the mishap that happened next. Jillian was walking past me just as I stood up and tripped over my chair and fell face first into her potatoes.

"Susan, you did that on purpose!" she yelled. "You are going to pay for that!"

Mr. Michaels came to Jillian's rescue. If I was pale before, I can't imagine what I looked like in that moment. Mr. Michaels escorted Jillian out of the lunchroom so she could clean herself off.

"You are going to pay for that!" The words echoed in my head. All the things Jillian did to me in the past worried me as I thought about how this accident would result in my future interactions with her. All of a sudden, I lost my appetite and just sat back down.

At the end of the school day, I had successfully made it on the bus without any incident. I sat next to Amber, and she told me how her day went. She went on and on about how they drew pictures and learned to write their names. I half listened as I continued to replay the incident that happened at lunch; I worried about what the rest of the school year would be like.

We arrived home and walked through the front door of the apartment building, where the broken lock required no key. The lock had been broken for who knows how long now. We walked along the dark, damp hallway as the cockroaches and mice scurried along the floor. During a short walk up the stairs to the third floor, we managed to avoid falling through the broken wooden steps. We arrived at our apartment. I slipped my key into the lock of the door marked 329.

"Mom, are you home?" I called out as I looked for her, but there was no sign of her. I walked over to the kitchen table to find a note:

Susan, pick up your brother from next door. I will be home later. There is bread on the counter, peanut butter in the cupboard, and jelly in the fridge.

I crumpled up the paper and threw it in the trash.

"Amber, change out of your school clothes and start your homework," I said in an overly motherly tone for a nine-year-old, and I headed for the door. "I am going next door to get Jonathan. Don't leave the apartment."

After picking up my brother, I started my daily routine: peanut butter and jelly for us all, help Amber with her homework, do my homework, and watch our evening programs. Then around eight o'clock I got us all ready for bed. Sometimes Mom was home; most times she came home long after we were asleep. This was one of the nights Mom was not home.

I woke up to the sound of the front door slamming shut and someone stumbling in, which I assumed was Mom. I held my breath as I hid in bed for a few minutes to listen for more clues. The keys hit a table, a chair scraped across the kitchen floor, and I heard the refrigerator door open. After knowing it was Mom and not someone breaking in, I cautiously got up and made my way to the kitchen.

"Mom, are you okay?" I asked her. I found her with her head and arm resting on refrigerator door, which was anchoring her in an upright position. I could tell that she was not awake. I carefully approached her. "Mom, wake up Mom." I gently gave her a shake. With that she woke up and gave me a glaring look.

"What?! Why are you out of bed? Go back to sleep," she snarled at me. "I am just tired." I could smell the alcohol on her breath and knew that she had been out drinking.

This had become a regular routine for her since Dad had left. We would come home from school and have to fend for ourselves. I would take care of my brother and sister, give them their baths, make sure they ate, did their homework, and get everyone to bed. Mom would come home late at night after we had all fallen asleep. She would always smell of alcohol and eventually stumble into bed. On a few occasions, when I had gone out to check on her, she had gotten upset with me and once she smacked me across the face for "questioning her," or "being out of bed," or whatever the reason was at the moment. Unfortunately, this is how I remember most of my childhood. Defeated, I went back to bed.

Don't move, I tell myself. I am lying as still as I can. I have pulled the sheets up over my face, as if this will hide me from the monster that lingers just outside my bedroom. I hear the low growling and sharp claws scraping on the door. I can feel heaviness on my chest. I am barely breathing. Sweat is pouring down my face. Tears puddle in the corners of my eyes. Don't breathe, I tell myself again. The growling is getting louder. I try to sink deeper into the mattress, but it's no use. I hear the door creak open; the monsters are coming closer, and I hear their heavy breathing. Don't breathe. Don't breathe. The monster is hovering over my bed, I feel the sheets get pulled, exposing me from my safety...

"NOOOOO!" I sprang up in my bed and screamed out. My sister and brother sat up in their beds. They were all too familiar with the nightmares. They stared at me for a few seconds to make sure I was okay before falling back to sleep.

I sat there just staring at the door. Wishing that someone existed in my life that would come and comfort me. Other kids my age had loving parents that came running into their room when their child had a nightmare. They would hug them and calm them down, tell them it would all be okay. But I knew that everything was not okay. No one was going to come into my room to comfort me or hold me until I fell back to sleep. There was no one for me to go to talk to about my nightmares, my battles with Jillian, or to get help with my mom. There was so much pressure on me to be the strong one so that I could hold our family together. I was the one that couldn't cry, because if I did, then everyone would know that I was falling apart. So I stayed strong day after day.

As for Jillian, the bully from school, I wish I could say that I had seen the last of her. She did make me pay for the lunchroom incident. She in fact continued to make my life miserable long beyond grammar school and all throughout high school.

Sadly, I have learned that there is a "Jillian" we all face. Often, I had to comfort my sister who had to face her own "Jillian." Amber and I would often stay up to talk after Jonathan fell asleep. I was tough and could handle Jillian picking on me. Amber was not as tough as me. Amber, crying, began telling me stories about how Ashley and her friends spread lies about her. They would bump into her in the hallway and cause her to drop all her books. They played pranks on her and tricked her into embarrassing herself. Amber did not respond well to attacks from her classmates. She came home crying almost every day. I watched as she began to close herself out from everyone around her. She barely talked to me anymore and would often close herself in our room and just cry. I tried to comfort her, but I didn't know how to help. I felt like I was in a losing battle.

Chapter Two: The Tormentors

The days turned into weeks, weeks turned into months, and months turned into years. Eventually we came to realize that Dad was not coming back. Jonathan, six years old and not knowing any better, made the mistake one day of asking Mom about this. Mom's response to Jonathan was cold.

"I don't know! What kind of man walks out on his family? We don't need him."

Jonathan ran out of the room crying. I looked at my mother in disbelief. I was almost thirteen years old. I had long ago learned that my mother had no intent of comforting us, so I slid out of my chair and went after Jonathan. I found him curled up on his bed weeping.

"I'm sorry, Jonathan. I know Daddy loves you very much." I tried to comfort him with my words, but I knew that the scar of our father leaving was thicker than words. I pulled Jonathan up to a sitting position and gave him a hug. "I love you, Jonathan. Mommy didn't mean it. She's just upset," I said, knowing that Mom was always upset and she did mean it.

Jonathan always recovered quickly from his meltdowns. In almost no time, he was back to his old self and we went back out to finish eating breakfast. The rest of the morning went without incident. We hopped on our bus and headed off to school. At this point, I had to take a second bus from Amber and Jonathan's school over to the middle school. I got off the bus at the middle school, only to find myself face to face with

Jillian, who now had a small army of other girls that were just like her.

"Oh man, Jillian, look what the cat just dragged in," the tall, blond girl next to Jillian announced, just loud enough to make sure that I heard her.

"I know. Do you see that blouse? She must have bought it from a homeless woman," Jillian snarled back. I heard the group of girls laughing as they walked into the building.

I put on my thick skin and threw my backpack over my shoulder and headed into school. At my locker, round two with Jillian and her posse began.

"Tammy, did you hear that Susan's father couldn't stand her *so* much that he just up and left the family?" Jillian looked over at me with a foul look, just daring me to say something back.

"Oh yeah, I heard that her mother is a raging alcoholic. She can't even hold down a job," Tammy shot back with an evil laugh.

My heart began to race and my face flushed. I clenched my fists to the point of pain in the palms of my hands. *Just ignore them*, I told myself. But how was I supposed to let them get away with talking about my family? I did not care what they said about me, but when they started to talk badly about my family, they were crossing a line. Was it true? Did my mom drink too much? Yes. Did she recently lose her job? Yes. Was it any of their business? NO! I was just about to give them a piece of my mind when the warning bell rang, letting us know we had just about a minute to get to class. This was just enough to dislodge my anger from me and what I might have done in response. I grabbed my books and walked in the opposite direction from Jillian and her clique.

Another day filled with classes. I managed to get through most the day without having to deal with Jillian and her snotty little friends. At lunch I did what I could to sit as far away from them as I could. Occasionally, I could hear them laughing and looking over at me, and I knew they were saying something that I preferred not to know.

Finally the day ended. All the students began to make their way to their lockers to gather their items and head off to where their next event was. As I looked around, I could see different lifestyles. As I looked to my right I saw a group of girls that were heading off to some sports practice or game. They were carrying what looked like soccer shoes, so I ventured to guess they were off to the soccer field.

I heard one of them say, "Camille, aren't you so excited about the game against the Panthers? We are so going to crush them!" They all gave a good laugh and were off to the soccer field.

Yup, soccer, I thought to myself.

I looked to my left and saw a group of boys. No doubt that they were football jocks. "Yo man, let's go do this!" one of the boys screamed out as they all gave each other high fives, as off they went to the football field.

Everywhere I looked there were seemingly normal kids with normal lives who were happy and enjoying life. Me, on the other hand, I was miserable! I felt like I had no purpose in life. My mom was an alcoholic. My dad left us. I spent most my days after school taking care of my brother and sister. *If this is the rest of my life, this sucks*, I thought to myself. I gathered my books and things I needed and stuffed them into my backpack. I headed for the door to catch my bus home; however, just outside the door I ran into the trouble (literally). In my rush to get to my bus, I wasn't quite looking where I was going and ran straight into Tammy, who was standing with Jillian.

"Watch where you are going *sleazy Susan*!" Tammy barked at me. This was a new name that they had started calling me over the last week or two. I hated it.

"Yeah sleazy Susan. What's the matter? You been drinking with your mom or something? Can't see where you're going?" Jillian chanted as they both began to laugh.

"Shut up!" I barked back at them as I tried to brush past them. Unfortunately, I didn't make it beyond a couple of steps when I felt something ram me from behind. I lost my balance and went flying face first into the ground. I felt something warm running down my face. I could feel the tears begin to well up in the corners of my eyes. Determined not to let them see me cry, I got up and ran toward my bus. I could hear them laughing as I ran away.

You are so stupid, Susan. You are such a coward. You can't even stand up for yourself or your family. The words rang in my head. Not their words, but something else. Something from within chanted these words. They were so loud that I didn't even hear what Tammy and Jillian were saying about me as I ran off.

I squinted my eyes and through my blurred vision I finally found my bus. I could still feel the blood running down my face from my nose. My right cheek was searing with pain. I tried to hide my face from the other kids. I managed to get past the driver and make my way to the back, where I found an empty seat. I uncovered my face and looked down at my blood-covered sweater. A girl about my age came and sat down next to me.

"You look like a mess," she said to me. "I saw what Jillian and Tammy did to you. They are so mean. My name is Margaret," the girl said to me as she pulled out some tissues from her backpack and handed them to me.

I just nodded my head in agreement as I tended to my bloody nose. We sat there quietly for the rest of the ride. When we reached the elementary school, Margaret and I parted ways. As Margaret turned around, she waved. "See you tomorrow," she said.

My nose had finally stopped bleeding as I found the bus that would take me home. I made my way to the back, where I found Jonathan and Amber. I didn't feel like getting into the drama of what happened, so I just told them I tripped and fell. When we got home, we found Mom in the living room, drinking. Normally when we get home, the house is empty. I am never quite sure where Mom is, so we just go about our day. Today, however, was different.

Chapter Three: A Broken Family

I could tell that Mom had already had a lot to drink, her eyes red and filled with bitterness and anger. She smelled of alcohol. As she crossed the room to get another bottle, she swayed and staggered, running into anything that was in her way. Anything and everything set her off.

"Mom, is everything okay?" I sheepishly asked from across the room.

"Yes, everything is fine! Just let me be!" she snapped back at me.

"Come on Amber and Jonathan," I said to them, nudging them toward the bedroom.

"I'm hungry," both whined. "Can't we get something to eat?"

"Later. Mom needs her space," I continued, directing them toward the bedroom. However, we all came to an abrupt stop when Mom spoke up.

"Give them something to eat!" Mom barked from the living room. "If they are hungry make them something to eat," she continued. She was now making her way toward us.

We sunk back as far as we could in an attempt to make ourselves disappear. With each step Mom took toward us, the tension in the room grew thicker. None of us had ever seen her this bad, nor did we know what to do.

"Answer me when I am talking to you!" came Mom's voice again. "You three are so ungrateful. You take and take and take.

It's your fault your father left. I should have just left with him."
Her words were like a slap across the face, leaving unseen
scars.

She had never talked to us this way before. It's not like this
was the first time that we had seen her drinking. It was more
like anger, even hatred. My mom's hand came up around my
chin, interrupting my thoughts.

"What happened to you? A little fighting, I suppose! I got a
call from your school. They said that you were fighting with
one of the girls there. She told them that you started the fight.
Is that true? Go figure, you are such a troublemaker," Mom
said as she squeezed tighter around my chin. My hands were
trembling, as was the rest of my body. I was frozen; no, I didn't
dare move, not even an inch. I could feel pain in my chest from
the lack of sucking in oxygen, for fear that if I would even
breathe it might set her off. But before I knew it, words were
coming out of my mouth. *No! What was I doing?*

"It wasn't my fault. I didn't do anything wrong," I blurted
out.

The stinging on my cheek was the response I got for my careless words. Amber and Jonathan's cheeks were glistening with
tears. I crumbled to the ground. Instantly, I felt Amber's arm
come around my neck as she hugged me. I could feel warmth
around my side, and quickly realized it was Jonathan. I felt
Amber's arms become forcefully unlocked from our embrace.
When I opened my eyes I saw Amber getting hurdled across
the room.

"Get away from her!" Mom yelled at Amber. Amber lost
her balance and fell backwards. She landed on her wrist, and I
heard it crack from across the room. She screamed in pain.

As I made my way over to Amber I could see that her arm
was broken just below her elbow. Mom took one look at us

28

and stumbled as she made her way out the front door. Once the door slam shut, I scrambled to my feet and headed for the phone.

"Hello. My sister, um…fell. Yes. No. No. We are at, um… at…" My brain had seemed to go numb. I couldn't think straight and our address didn't come to mind. "Um, 6811 South Union Street, by West 68th Street. Apartment, apartment… um…3…2…ummm…it's apartment 3…2…9." My voice was shaking. I hung up the phone and, after what seemed like forever, a knock came at the door. There was a bustle of bodies that made their way through the door. First came the firefighters, and then came the ambulance people. They made their way over to my sister and started to wrap her arm up.

"Where are your parents?" I heard one of them say.

"At wa…work." The words just tumbled out of my mouth. I gave a look of warning to Amber and Jonathan not to say otherwise.

"Did you call them to let them know what happened?" a woman asked.

"Ummm…no…I mean, yes. We couldn't get ahold of Mom. Her phone is off." I tried to keep my voice calm as I lied about this.

Two of the workers gave each other a funny look, and I could feel the butterflies in my stomach. They began to confer with each other and I couldn't quite hear what they were saying. A few minutes later, one of the firefighters left the room. I had a bad feeling about this. Why did I call them? How could I make them go away? The same woman who asked where my parents were must have sensed my nervousness. She looked over at me and gave me a big smile.

"It's okay, sweetheart. Everything will be okay." She gave me another smile, but somehow I still felt like something was wrong.

Within a matter of minutes there were two police officers at our door. My stomach began to turn. What was going on? I was so confused. How could I let this happen? What was I supposed to do? Before I could decide how I should respond, the medics brought my sister to the ambulance.

"All right, kids, we are going to take your sister to the hospital. We need to have you go with the officers, and they are going to continue to try to contact your parents," one of the ambulance drivers said.

I couldn't help but feel like something was still wrong. How could I make this right? I knew that my mother had her phone with her, but I didn't want them to call her. I didn't know what would happen if they reached her. She was so drunk when she left. Would they arrest her? Would we ever see her again? Did I want her to get arrested? Did I care if we ever saw her again? I couldn't hold back my emotions anymore. My stomach was turning, my mind was swirling, and my head was aching. I couldn't hold back the tears anymore and began to cry. Johnny took a cue from me and started crying.

"What's the matter? Is everything okay?" the one officer looked back at us and asked. "Don't be afraid. Everything will be okay."

"I'm...I'm...okay," I stumbled. "I just wish my mom was here," I lied. The truth was that I didn't want her here. She was the reason we were in this situation. I hated her. Well, I loved her, but I hated her. Everything was so messed up.

We gave the officers Mom's number. We didn't have much of a choice. He tried a few times, but it kept going to her voice mail. Finally, the officer left a message, letting her know what happened and that they were going to bring us to the hospital.

When we got to the hospital, they allowed my brother and I

to go into the room with my sister. The police officers, ambulance drivers, and someone else that we didn't know were all in the hallway outside the door talking. I couldn't hear what they were saying. They kept looking over at us with this look of pity. Eventually, one of the women that we did not know came into the room to talk to us.

"Hi, my name is Lucille. I am a social worker here at the hospital. Do you know what a social worker is?" she asked as she looked closely at the three of us. The woman was about the same height as my mom. Not too tall, but not short either. She had blond hair, which she had bunched up in the back of her head. She didn't look scary. I had heard of social workers before. Everything I heard about them, though, was bad.

"Um, I don't know. No…um…not really," Amber stammered. I didn't say anything.

I knew what social workers do. They take children from their parents. I was starting to feel even worse than I did before. I pulled Jonathan close to me and gave him a gentle squeeze to try to comfort him.

"Well, a social worker is someone who helps people with their situations. They help to make things better," Lucille said as she gave us all a half-smile. "I want to see if we can try calling your parents to let them know that you are here. Do you have their phone numbers?"

"Daddy left us," Amber said with tears in her eyes. "We don't have any way to get ahold of him."

"I have my mom's cell phone number," I said as I tried to change the subject. "The police officer tried to call, but she didn't answer. He left a message so that she wouldn't worry about us if she came home and we were not there."

"Well, I am sure that she is on her way," Lucille said with a gentle smile. "Now, let's talk about what happened. Here, sit down," Lucille said to my brother and myself as she moved a chair closer to us. "Let's start with how Amber hurt her arm."

"She tripped over something in the livin…" I started to say, but at the same time, Amber said, "I fell off my bike."

"Hmm. Seems to me that you were riding your bike in the living room and fell off of it because you tripped. Does that sound about right?" Lucille gave us a smile again and a gentle laugh. "It is important that you be honest with me so that I can help."

"She didn't mean it…really she didn't," Amber blurted out. "I made her upset. It is all my fault." She began to cry uncontrollably.

"Amber!" I yelled. I couldn't hold back any longer. She was going to mess up everything. This woman didn't care about us. She just wanted to get in our business and have us sent to some foster home.

"Sorry, Suzie," Amber said in a shaky, teary voice. "I didn't mean to mess up again. I never say the right things."

"Hey, how about you two go and get a snack from the vending machine." Lucille handed a couple of dollars to me. "Take your brother so he can pick something special out."

"No, thank you," I said with a bluntness that took Lucille by surprise. "I would rather stay here with Amber." I was going to stand my ground. She wasn't going to get rid of me that easily.

"Suzie, pleeeease! I want to get something special. Can we go, please, pretty please?" Jonathan begged. Something about his innocence was enough to make me break, and I agreed. Before leaving, I gave Amber a look that said keep your mouth shut.

I wasn't gone long, but when I got back to the room where Amber was, the social worker was gone and the doctor was there. He was explaining to the social worker that he would need to have her arm x-rayed, but that he would need to have her parents sign and give permission for medical treatment. I couldn't believe my sight as my mother stumbled into the room. There was no way Mom could hide her bloodshot eyes and the alcohol on her breath.

"Where is my daughter?" my mother asked, slurring her words as she stumbled into the room.

"Ma'am. Why don't we go out in the hallway and talk?" the doctor said as he gently took ahold of my mom's arm to redirect her toward the door.

"Let go of me!" my mom screamed as she yanked her arm away from the doctor. "You have no right to tell me what to do!"

"Ma'am, I think it would be better for your children if you would come talk to me outside." He was now blocking the path between her and us.

Just then, a nurse and security guard came into the room, and all of a sudden, before our eyes, the security guard had wrestled Mom to the ground.

Chapter Four: A Divided House

The image of my brother and sister being put in the back of a stranger's car, and me being put in a different car, is a memory I will never get rid of. How could I let them split us up? How could I have ever let these strangers tear our family apart?

"Susan…please stop them! Susan, don't let them take us!" I could hear my sister and brother crying out to me from the other car.

"Let me go! You can't do this. This isn't fair. We didn't do anything wrong. Get out of my way!" I shouted at the strange woman who was standing between my siblings and me.

"I'm sorry, sweetheart. I know this isn't your fault and it's not fair. They will make arrangements for you to see each other. There are no foster families that will accept three children. We were able to get a family to take both your sister and brother, but they couldn't take three children," the woman said to me. I know she told me her name, but I didn't care what it was, nor did I remember it.

The woman guided me into the car and shut me in. I felt like a caged animal, trapped. On the drive to this new place that I would be forced to stay at, the enemy, Ms. Whatever-her-face, who I am going to call Ms. "Ogre" since that is what she was— a mean, family breaking-upping ogre—Ms. Ogre was blabbing on about something or another. I heard about every tenth word. "…You will like her.…she is one of our best…" Blah, blah, blah.

We arrived in a quiet neighborhood where a woman was standing on a small front stoop of an old apartment complex. I rolled myself out of the car and sluggishly made my way toward the steps. I knew there was no point of fighting the system. I knew too many friends that had gone through this, and they never won.

"This is Ms. Smith. Ms. Smith, this is the girl we talked about, Susan. Susan has had a hard day. I'm sure she could use some rest," Ms. Ogre said, and she was off to ruin some other family's life.

Ms. Smith led the way up several flights of stairs until we reached the third floor. When we entered through the apartment, we first entered into a hallway that had a closet to the left. As we walked on, we passed a small kitchen and dining area. Ms. Smith stated that this was the kitchen area, as if the refrigerator and stove didn't already give that away. She told me to eat whatever I wanted and to make myself at home. We continued past a small area with an ugly, flower-patterned couch. I would have thought that Ms. Smith was in her sixties instead of her late thirties from the look of the apartment's decor. We made our way to the back of the apartment, which didn't take much time, as the apartment was quite small. Ms. Smith pointed to the door on the left and indicated that this was her bedroom. She pointed to the door on the right and stated that this was my room.

"Susan, I will be in the living room watching television if you want to join me. I know this is a lot to handle. I would understand if you would rather get unpacked and settle in," Ms. Smith said as she gave a warm smile and headed out of the room.

This wasn't exactly what I decided to do, to lock myself in this "prison" that the stupid social worker sent me to stay in. I didn't plan on being here long, as I was going home. There was no reason to unpack. I sat in a strange bedroom on an unfamiliar bed. My heart pounded, my mind was numb, and I felt the color draining from my face.

Sometime in the evening there came a knock on the door. I snarled, "Go away."

"Susan, it's Ms. Smith. I have some dinner for you."

"I'm not hungry. Just leave me alone!" I barked back.

"You have to eat something. I am going to leave it outside the door. Come and get it when you are hungry," she said. I heard her put a plate down and then heard her steps as she walked away.

I felt my stomach growl and the gnawing feeling was a mixture of hunger with nervousness and anger. My body felt lifeless and cold and I felt a shiver run through me. I could feel the sadness in my chest screaming and yelling, wanting out from the prison I locked it in. Why couldn't I cry? Why couldn't I feel anything? What was wrong with me? I couldn't stand the thought of my mother being angry with me. When we went home, I was sure to get a beating. I just stared at the door. The silence was deafening. Then I heard some footsteps downstairs, a car alarm outside, and voices just below my window. *Oh, I am so hungry*, I thought to myself.

I pushed myself up off the bed with what little strength I had left and shuffled to the door. I paused and listened before opening the door, just a crack, and peeked out. The hallway was empty.

"Yes. I am not sure, Myrtle. Yes, about an hour ago. Well, I couldn't say no." I could hear my "foster mother" talking on the phone just down the hall. I swung the door open, grabbed the tray of food, and closed the door swiftly behind me. The last thing I wanted was to have some strange woman trying to ask questions.

In a matter of minutes, I had gobbled down the turkey sandwich and stuffed fists full of chips into my mouth. My stomach still felt empty, but the thought of asking for more food just made me sick to my stomach.

I don't understand why I am here. I don't understand what we did wrong. Why are we being punished? I should have protected my brother and sister. I wonder if they are okay. If I only knew where they were now I would go get them and we could all run away together.

A knock at the door interrupted my thoughts.

"Susan, there is a call for you. It's your sister and brother," the woman said.

I jumped out of bed and ran across the room toward the door. As I reached the door, I stumbled on something and tumbled across the floor. I quickly got up and brushed myself off. I felt embarrassed. I am not sure why. No one was there to see me fall. I pushed the thought aside, opened the door, and grabbed the phone right out of the woman's hand. Once I had the phone, I slammed the door closed before the woman had anything else to say. I know that I was being rude, but I didn't care. I didn't plan on staying long.

"Hello? Amber…are you okay? Where are you? Is Jonathan okay?" I spit out so many questions that Amber didn't seem to know where to start, so she started with crying. I could hear the sadness in her voice.

"Suzie…Suzie…I don't like it here. I want to go home." Amber's voice trembled as she spoke. I could barely hear her. She was whispering. Why was she whispering?

My mind went blank. For a brief second I didn't have words to say. I wanted to say, "Don't worry, I am coming to get you," but I knew that I couldn't make a promise that I couldn't keep.

A WALK WITHIN

So instead, I just told her everything would work out and to stay strong. This was probably a lie, too, but one that was less harmful than me coming to get them.

"Suzie, the house smells funny. I am afraid of Mr. and Mrs. Stevens. They are mean. They yell a lot. They don't know that I called you. The woman that dropped us off here gave me your number," Amber said in a weak and defeated voice.

"Amber, just hang in there. I will fix everything. I just need some time. I will not let anyone hurt you and Jonathan." If that were only the case, since no sooner did the words come out of my mouth than Amber's foster parents found her talking on the phone.

"What are you doing? Did I give you permission to talk on the phone? Give me that!" I heard a smacking noise and the phone went dead. I frantically tried to remember if I had Amber's phone number, but quickly realized I never asked for it. How stupid! Stupid, stupid, stupid! Why didn't I ask for the number?

Anything I was feeling about the woman I was staying with or my wish not to interact with her instantly left me. I ran out of my room and into the hallway and down the stairs. In the midst of my running, I ran smack into Ms. Smith.

"My sister…brother…phone…smack…help!" I couldn't get words to come out, and they were making no sense.

"Hold on child, you're not making any sense," the woman said.

"My sister…she called. Her foster parents didn't know. She snuck and called. I think they hit her. Please, you need to help. You need to call someone." I managed to have a few words tumble out of my mouth that had logic to them.

"Sweetheart, I am sure they are fine. Did she give you a phone number, we can try giving them a call," the woman said.

There was something about her voice that was soothing.

"No. I didn't get a chance to ask. Please, we need to make sure they are okay," I begged as I tugged at her shirt.

"Let me try calling the social worker. Maybe they can send someone over there to check on them." I don't know why, but all of a sudden this woman seemed so different, and I no longer wanted to hide myself away from her.

"Um, yes, hi…this is Ms. Smith. Can I talk to Mrs. Hampton? No, it's not an emergency, but it's urgent and very important. Well, can you have her call me back? Thank you." Ms. Smith, so that was her name. She hung up the phone and gave a sigh. "I'm sorry, dear, but Mrs. Hampton is out of the office."

"No, we need to do something. Can't you talk to someone else? What can we do?" I cried out in anger.

"Sweetheart, all we can do now is wait for Mrs. Hampton to call us back. They told me that she will call back soon." Ms. Smith stood there looking at me. There was something different about her. I didn't know what it was. I couldn't quite put my finger on it. "Let's go and sit in the living room and we can talk about this some more." I don't know why, but I didn't fight her on this. My heart was beating rapidly, my mind was racing, and my whole body felt like Jell-O.

In the living room, Ms. Smith sat down in a plump green chair. She pointed to a couch that was next to her and asked me to sit down. I obeyed. I am not sure what it was about her, but it seemed calming and soothing when I was around her. We just sat there quietly for what seemed like forever. Finally, I was the one that broke the silence.

"It's my fault," I said as I looked down at the floor. I shuffled my feet across the carpet.

"What's your fault?" Ms. Smith responded. Her voice was gentle.

A WALK WITHIN

"Why I am here. Why Amber and Jonathan are in that horrible house. Why my dad left us. Why my mom drinks too much. Everything...everything is my fault. I am the reason." I couldn't hold it in anymore. It all escaped from the prison that I had it all locked away in. The words, the tears, the anger; it all came pouring out.

"Can you explain to me how all those things are your fault? It seems to me that those are all things that are out of your control," said Ms. Smith.

"If I was never born my parents wouldn't have gotten married. If...if...I don't know. It's just all my fault." I didn't know how to process it all. The phone ringing interrupted my stream of self-hating thoughts. I jumped up and darted for the phone, but before I picked it up, a thought came to me: *Don't pick it up or you might also be smacked like your sister was.* I looked back at Ms. Smith with a questioning look.

"Go ahead, honey, you can answer it," she said.

"Hello? Mrs. Hampton?" I asked the question before the other person was even able to say hello.

"Susan, is that you?" Mrs. Hampton replied.

"Oh, Mrs. Hampton, I need you to check on my sister and brother. Please, I need your help. I am afraid that they are unsafe where they are. I was on the phone...and I heard someone get hit and the phone went dead...and...oh, please, help them!" I was back to having the words just tumble out of my mouth.

"Susan, calm down. Take a deep breath. I just talked to Amber and her foster parents. Everything is okay," Mrs. Hampton said, which somehow didn't reassure me.

"I want to see them. When can I see them? Can I have their phone number? This is not fair. Why can't they come and live here?" I threw question after question at her.

"Susan, is Ms. Smith there? Can I talk to her?" Mrs. Hampton asked.

"But, but…fine." I didn't have the energy to fight anymore. I handed the phone over to Ms. Smith. "Here, she wants to talk to you."

Ms. Smith gradually made her way over to the phone and gave me a reassuring half hug.

"Hello, Mrs. Hampton. Yes, I understand. Susan is really worried about her brother and sister. Is there any way that we can set up a visit sometime soon? Yes, hang on while I get a pen and paper. Susan, dear, can you get me a pen and piece of note paper from over in that container there?" she said as she pointed toward a small desk that was over in the corner. I quickly grabbed the pen and paper and rushed back to where Ms. Smith was standing. While she continued talking, I paced back and forth, biting my nails. Her conversation with Mrs. Hampton seemed to go on forever. When she finally hung up I couldn't take it any more.

"What did she say? Is she going to set up a visit? Did she give you the phone number for where they are staying?" I asked question after question without waiting for an answer.

"Susan, let's go into the living room and continue talking," Ms. Smith said as she put her arm around my shoulders and guided me back into the living room. There was something alarming about her tone that made me uneasy.

As we sat in the living room, Ms. Smith explained to me that both her home and the home that Amber and Jonathan were staying in were only temporary. She explained that we would all be in these homes for only a couple of weeks while they looked for a permanent placement. Ms. Smith shared that the agency that Mrs. Hampton worked for was going to try to find a foster home that could place all of us together, but there are not many homes that are able to do this.

"Why can't we all just stay here?" I asked in a pleading voice.

"Susan, I would love to have you all live here. However, the agency will only allow me to have one youth here. There are not enough rooms and, well, it's complicated. I also can only have children stay with me on a temporary basis while they look for a long-term placement. There are lots of children that need a safe place to stay while they find a long-term plan. I know you do not understand this, and I hope one day that you do, but that is how it is." Ms. Smith looked at me with tears in her eyes. I could tell that she really cared. I still haven't been able to figure out what made her so different. But it didn't matter because in a couple of weeks I would be moved to a new home, with a new foster parent or parents, and it wouldn't matter anymore. My father didn't love me, my mother didn't love me, and now Ms. Smith didn't want or love me. What difference did it make anyway? Who needed love anyway? All that it leads to is heartache and pain.

And so, the journey began where I ended up in a long string of foster homes, eventually being forced to leave them due to bad behavior on my part.

Chapter Five: The Flight of Brokenness

It was the day of my move from Ms. Smith's home to my next foster home. I packed all my belongings into the one suitcase I had and headed downstairs. Mrs. Hampton was at the bottom of the stairs looking up at me with pity in her eyes. I hated that look. Don't pity me. If you don't care enough about me to rescue me from the grips of heartache, don't feel sorry for me. That will not solve anything. Ms. Smith gave me a hug, which I returned with a cold and half-hearted pat on her back, and quickly squirmed from her warm and tender arms. My heart sank as I walked out the door, but it would be years before I would understand why.

"Susan, I know this is hard. Please understand that Ms. Smith did not want to let you go. The system is in place for a reason," Mrs. Hampton said in a sad, weepy voice.

"I don't care. Can we just please not talk?" I retorted back.

"Susan, I know you are hurt, but pushing away those who are trying to help you will not accomplish anything," she continued.

"Help me? Help me? You have got to be kidding!" I shouted as color flooded my face.

We drove the rest of the way in silence. It felt like the distance between Ms. Smith's house and my next foster home was hours rather than minutes.

"This is where you will be staying," Mrs. Hampton said as she opened the car door and motioned for me to get out. "This is Ms. Chambers, Ms. Chambers this is Susan. Here is all the information we talked about on the phone—emergency phone numbers and the contact information for Susan's siblings. I will be back in a couple of weeks to check on how things are going."

Ms. Chambers gave me a fake smile, as if she was glad to see me. But there was just something about her that I didn't trust. Something was just off. I quickly found out what that was.

"You come back here, Susan! You will not disrespect me like that! Susan…Susan!" Ms. Chambers ranted at me as I walked away from her.

"You are not my mother! You can't tell me what to do!" I shouted back.

"How dare you talk to me like that, you ungrateful little witch!" Ms. Chambers was fast behind me and my heart began to beat faster as I picked up my pace.

"Get away from me you old hag." I no sooner got the words out of my mouth when Ms. Chambers caught my arm, spun me around, and I felt a stinging sensation on my cheek. I was stunned and didn't know whether to be angry, afraid, or just cry.

"I am going and you can't stop me. You have no right to lay your hands on me. I am going to call Mrs. Hampton and report you, you…you…old hag!" I was now screaming as loud as my lungs would let me. I could feel the sensation of myself fall backwards and my backside come in contact with the floor, before I realized that Ms. Chambers had just shoved me to the ground. It all happened so quickly.

"You just try to tell anyone about this, you ungrateful brat, and you will just end up in another foster home, and they will care even less about you than I do!"

I sat there cuddling myself in a ball wanting so desperately to cry. Why wouldn't the stupid tears just come out? Why couldn't I feel anything besides anger? Ahhhh! I just wanted to scream, but my feelings just welled up inside. I got myself to my feet and stormed into my bedroom. I changed into the only outfit I had that was worthy of being called "party attire" and climbed out my window. I calmed myself down and headed for the party at Maggie's house. Maggie was a new friend I made, and tonight she had a few friends over while her mother was out of town.

***

"Come on, Susan. Just try it. It tastes just like peaches. You'll like it," Maggie chanted. "Just take a sip."

I was at my first party, and I had never had alcohol before. I had seen what it did to my mother and didn't like what I saw, but I didn't want my friends to think I was afraid. Besides, after the confrontation I just had with Ms. Chambers and all the anger and hurt I had inside, I just wanted something to take it all away.

"Fine, just a sip," I said as I took a sip...then another, and another. "Hmm, this is really good," I said for the tenth time, as I slurred my words. "Whoaw it dowas tass juss like peaches," I said about two hours later. "I juss can't get enouf of dis stuff."

"Wow, Susan. Maybe you have had enough," Maggie said as she wrestled me for the glass I was holding. I didn't have the strength to fight her off. Besides, it didn't take long before I was passed out on the floor.

Stomp. Slam. Chirp! *Oh so loud. Stop the noise.* Everything was echoing in my head. *Where am I? Oh, my aching head. Eww, what is that awful smell? Ick, what is this wet stuff?*

"Gross! Who threw up on me?" I shouted as I rolled myself up off the floor and out of the slimy pile of vomit that I had apparently been sleeping in.

My head throbbed and I didn't dare raise my voice again. I looked over at the couch and saw Emily sprawled out. Denis was flopped over on a recliner just next to her.

"Susan, you threw up on yourself. Now shut up, we're trying to sleep. My head is killing me," Maggie grumbled from her bedroom.

Another door slammed just outside of the apartment and the echo of stomping feet down the hall indicated that someone was heading out. I managed to make my way to the bathroom and stripped off my soiled clothes. As I turned the water on, the pipes rattled and the water began to pour out of the dingy faucet. The tub was covered in dirt and grime, but at this point, I didn't care. I let the hot water run over my sore aching body until it started to run cold. As I got out of the shower, I heard the front door to the apartment open and slam shut.

"Maggie, what in the world happened here?" I heard Maggie's mother yelling. *Oh the pounding, achy pain in my head. Make her stop!*

I heard a thump and shuffling feet. I could only assume Maggie had rolled herself out of bed and made her way into the living room. I had no idea what was going to happen. Maggie's mom was supposed to be out of town. She had trusted that her sixteen-year-old daughter would have behaved while she was gone, but instead she threw a party, where myself and four of our friends drank until we got sick or passed out or both. I hadn't thought this through, but since I threw up on my clothes, I didn't have anything to put on after my shower. I wrapped a towel around myself and sheepishly made my way out to the living room. At this point, everyone was in an upright position and Maggie's mother, Ms. Harborfield, was scolding us.

"Get in here and sit down young lady!" she ordered as I made my appearance in the room. "What is wrong with you all? I don't know what to say! I am going to have to call your parents."

A WALK WITHIN

Yeah, well go right ahead and do that. Not like they will care.
Mom is too busy getting plastered and Dad up and ran away.
Besides, my mother let them take me away and hasn't bothered
to come get us. Anyways, she'll have to call the old hag, Ms.
Chambers, and who cares what she thinks anyway?

Ms. Harborfield started making calls to parents and making arrangements for them to come pick us up. When she got to me, she asked for my parents' number.

"Here is the number to Ms. Chambers. You can tell her whatever you want, but she won't care. She's just out to get a check from the government for housing me," I said in a snarky tone as I wrote down Ms. Chambers' number.

Ms. Harborfield gave me a surprised look. It took her a moment to recover before she dialed the number I gave her.

"Hello, is this Ms. Chambers? I have Susan here with me. I came home and found her along with some of her friends and my daughter passed out and drunk from drinking all night. I just thought you should know. Can you please come pick her up? All right, thank you, I will see you soon." Ms. Harborfield hung the phone. "I don't understand it. She sounded very worried about you. You should really treat adults better. After seeing how you have behaved here last night, it's a wonder if she will even let you stay there."

They are all alike. Adults are all alike. They don't care about
us. They just treat us all the same, like we are worthless and
have no feelings. I am sick of it. If I left this earth today, no one
would even miss me or notice I was gone.

I didn't have the energy or desire to fight. I just let the words leave the bloody wounds of my soul. Besides, what is one more wound or scar to an already beaten and broken soul? The damage started long ago and there is no escaping it, so I might as well just accept it.

It didn't take long for the old hag to show up. She was so phony right from the start.

"Oh Susan, how could you do this? I was so worried about you. I didn't know what to do." Ms. Chambers came over to me and gave me a hug. My entire body became paralyzed with anger and fear. Something told me that if I fought her, she would just beat on me some more. Ms. Harborfield gave me a look that said, "See? I told you she cared about you," which I just ignored.

The air in the car was stifling, and with each breath I could feel the heaviness on my chest. I feared for the time when we arrived home. Despite the front I put on in the presence of my friends and Ms. Harborfield, I was terrified of how Ms. Chambers would respond. After the incident from yesterday, I didn't know what she was capable of.

When we got into the house and out of sight of any witnesses, the battle began. Ms. Chambers gave me another smack across the face. She grabbed my arm so hard that it left an impression on my skin. She dragged me up to my room, shoved me down onto the floor, and slammed the door behind her. When I turned to the window to escape, I had found it nailed shut. I ran to the door for my escape and found it wouldn't open.

"Let me out of here! You can't keep me locked in here forever," I shouted and beat on the door. I continued to pound my fists on the door until my knuckles began to bleed and I had no more strength left in my body. I crumbled into a heap on the floor, and in my state of exhaustion, fell asleep.

I woke up several hours later with an intense urgency to empty my bladder. I tried to open the door again, but found it was still locked. I pounded on it again and yelled out that I had to use the bathroom, but there was no response. I did this for an hour before I couldn't hold it in anymore and I could feel the warmth running down my legs. I cleaned myself up as best I could and changed. I was so embarrassed and ashamed. I could feel the welled up emotions of sadness buried deep in my heart, but there it would remain. I wanted to cry. I wanted to let it all out, but I couldn't. I needed to remain in control.

Several hours later as I lay crumbled on my floor, I felt my stomach growling with hunger. When was the last time I had eaten? I couldn't even remember?

The next morning I heard scraping on the outside of my door and footsteps walking the opposite direction. I cautiously made my way to the door, which I found unlocked. I looked down the hall in both directions before I made my way out.

The first thing I did in my new freedom was run to the bathroom and jump in the shower. I tried to scrub away the filth and smell of yesterday, but no matter how hard I scrubbed, I just didn't feel clean. After I scrubbed my skin raw, I fumbled out of the shower and grabbed a towel to dry off. The soft fluffy towel felt like sandpaper on my raw skin.

The bathroom door swung open and Ms. Chambers stormed in. I stood there wrapped in my towel, the only protective layer between the old hag and myself.

"Hmm, feeling nice and clean are you?" she said with a smug voice and a cigarette in her hand. "I'll teach you to respect me if it kills me," she continued as she crept into my personal space. "Nothing to say? No calling me names?"

"Please get away from me," I said with a quiver in my voice.

"Oh, she speaks," Ms. Chambers chanted. Just then I felt a burning sensation on my thigh. "Don't you dare disrespect me!" she continued as she removed her lit cigarette from my thigh. All I could do was let out a whimper.

The burning from cigarettes, being pushed down to the

ground and the smacking around continued for months. Ms. Chambers had beaten me into submission. I was too afraid to tell anyone about this, as I figured if this was how all foster homes were, the next one might be worse. So I just continued in my submissive state of discontent. I barely had any contact with my brother and sister. I was glad that they were in a safe home, which they reported to be doing well in.

I didn't want to bring any of the trouble I was faced with into their lives, so I kept my distance from them, to the point that I barely had any contact with them at all. I continued to stuff my feelings down deeper and deeper by drinking, and eventually got into doing some various types of drugs. I went from guy to guy, sleeping with each one of them. It was my only escape from the hell I was living in.

My behavior had caused many of my foster parents to give up on me. No big surprise there, though. Adults can't be counted on for anything. I bounced around from foster home to foster home. Several times I had ended up back at Ms. Smith's home for a week or two temporary stay while they worked on convincing the "long-term" foster parents to take me in. I didn't understand why I couldn't just stay with Ms. Smith. Who cares if the rules say she can only do temporary foster care? Who cares about rules at all? I certainly didn't.

***

When I turned eighteen years old, I "aged out" of foster care. My mother was still a mess, and I had barely any contact with her. Who knows where my father was, and really I didn't care. My brother and sister were settled with a nice foster home after they were moved from the first home they were in. I maintained a distance from them as much as I could. I knew my life was a mess, and I wanted to protect them from being influenced or impacted by the way my life was unraveling.

***

A WALK WITHIN

When was the last time I had seen Ms. Smith? I think it has been about a year. How many foster parents have I gone through over the past six years? I just turned nineteen years old and my life is going nowhere. Billy, what is he, guy number ten...no twelve...I can't even remember anymore. He is just one more guy I have moved in with in order to have somewhere to sleep and eat.

I let my mind continue to wander as I drifted off as I fell asleep.

Chapter Six: A Broken Soul

"Billy…wake up, Billy. I'm hungry. Go and get us some food," I said to the guy lying next to me. I guess you can call him a boyfriend of sorts: one of many guys in a long chain of them, all of which I had ended up sleeping with at some point or another.

"If you're hungry go get your own food. I have a headache and feel like crap," Billy barked at me in his usual careless tone. "While you are at it, you can get me something to eat too," he said as he rolled back over and fell asleep.

Good-for-nothing piece of…whatever. I need to do whatever I can to make sure I don't lose him. He is the best thing I have going for me. I just want someone to love me. I want someone to take care of me. I can't mess this up. I should have never slept with Billy…

My thoughts trailed off as I threw on my clothes from off the dingy floor in dark room and grabbed my purse. I left the small loft, only to walk out into the streets with police sirens blaring at me, scattered bottles of empty bourbon along the roadside, and a bunch of bums begging for money. I kept my head down and looked at my feet as I hurriedly made my way to the corner store two and a half blocks up the street. I rushed into the store and grabbed a couple of hot dogs and sodas. I walked up and down the aisle that had the feminine products in it, which sat right next to the pregnancy tests. I did a walk by and glanced at these items. I walked over to the next aisle pretending like

I was looking for something else. I circled back around to the aisle with the pregnancy tests. I didn't want anyone to know I was buying it. I was so embarrassed.

When was the last time I had my period? I can't even remember. Was it a month ago? No, maybe two months? What am I going to do? Billy is going to leave me.

I grabbed the pregnancy test box and rushed up to the counter with all my items. I tried to hide the pregnancy test box between my sodas and hot dogs so no one would see what I was buying.

Why didn't I just tell Billy to use protection? Why didn't I tell them all to use protection? I never wanted to have sex in the first place. Why did I allow them to talk me into this?

"That will be $12.96," the cashier said. However, my mind was elsewhere and I didn't even remember that I was standing at the register.

"What?" I said as I snapped back to reality.

"Your total. It will be $12.96," he repeated. He was looking at me with a judgmental gaze.

I know he was judging me for the stupid pregnancy test. What business was it of his anyway?

I gave him a twenty that I had stolen from Billy's wallet and grabbed my change and items and got out of there as fast as I could. I rushed back to the loft without looking up from my feet. To look up meant begging for money or a snide remark from those wandering the street. Back in the safety of the dingy, cold, and unwelcoming loft, I grabbed the pregnancy test out from the bag and hid it inside the lining of my pants.

A WALK WITHIN

The last thing I want to do is have Billy see this. I can't afford to have him walk out on me now.

I put the food down on the kitchen counter and made my way into the bathroom. I pulled out the box and opened it, my hands shaking. I dropped the box on the floor three times before I managed to get the stupid thing open. I quickly read the directions and sat there impatiently as I waited to see what the little white plastic stick would tell me.

I am so stupid. How could I have let myself get to this place? Billy is going to leave me. What am I going to do? I don't even have a job. I have barely any money. I have nowhere to live. Now my entire life circumstances can change based on what this stupid little white plastic thing says on it.

I sat there for what felt like an eternity and finally, after taking several deep breaths, picked up the test and to see what it said. In a state of confusion and anxiousness, I didn't know what two lines meant. Does that mean I'm pregnant? Does that mean I'm not pregnant? Why can't it just say yes or no? I fumbled for the directions and looked for the section that gave the answer to if I was pregnant or not. I found the picture that showed the two lines and next to it, it read "pregnant."

It can't be. How am I going to tell Billy? Maybe I don't have to. Maybe I can just go to the clinic down the street and he will never have to know. Can I do that? This is a life that is inside of me, isn't it? Will people know what I did?

I sat in the bathroom and just stared at the test in my hand. My whole life had just felt like it turned upside down. It didn't feel any different now that I knew that there was a baby growing inside of me, but now I knew it was there and I began to feel sick to my stomach. I turned around and fell to my knees and began throwing up everything that managed to still be in my stomach.

I need a drink. Drink...oh man, I can't drink. What will that do to the baby? What does it matter anyway? If I go to the clinic and have it taken care of, it will not matter what I drink or do to my body. I feel like an unwelcome guest invaded my body. I didn't ask for this. I never wanted to have children. I would just mess them up like my parents did.

The pounding on the door interrupted my thoughts.

"Susan, what in the world are you doing in there? I need to get in there. Get your ungrateful behind out of there," Billy barked at me from the other side of the door.

"Give me a minute. I am almost done," I said back to him with a weak voice. I found a towel and wiped my face off. I pulled myself up off the bathroom floor and made my way over to the sink. I splashed some cold water on my face and tried to shake off the anxiousness and headed out of the bathroom. I made my way to the edge of the bed before all the drama of the morning's event overtook me. When Billy came out from the bathroom, I couldn't hold in my emotions any longer and I began to cry. My entire body began to go into a convulsion-like state as the years of pent-up sadness, exhaustion, hurt, and pain poured out of me.

"What is your problem, Susan? What in the world has gotten into you? I can't deal with this. You are such a mess. Pull yourself together," Billy said as he walked past me and went into the kitchen and grabbed the hot dog I had purchased for myself. Apparently, he had already eaten his and now moved on to eating mine.

"I'm pregnant," I blurted out. I hadn't intended on saying anything; however, the words just came flooding out from nowhere.

"What? You better not be! I thought you were taking birth control. How could you have let this happen? I am not raising no baby. You know what, just get out of here. I can't stand to look at you now," Billy grabbed my arm and forcefully dragged me across the room toward the front door.

"No, Billy. I'm sorry. I'll take care of it. Please don't do this. Billy, please," I said as I tried to wrestle myself free from Billy's grip.

"Susan, it's over. Just get out of here. Only someone so stupid could let themselves get pregnant. I bet the baby is not even mine. Who else have you been sleeping around with?" Billy shoved me out the door and slammed it behind me.

I stood outside with tears pouring down my face, slamming my fists against his door.

"Please, Billy. Please. Don't do this. I am sorry. I will take care of it. Please don't do this. I don't have anywhere to go. Please...I love you...Billy..." I slid down the door and sat there, letting the numbness make its way back into my soul.

At nineteen years old, I'm pregnant and now homeless. I don't have any money for the clinic, even if I wanted to go there. What was I thinking? Maybe I can go home. Home, such a funny thought. Where is home? I don't have one of those anymore.

I stumbled to my feet and started to walk. Where I was going, I had no idea. So I just walked. I took a right here and a left there. Mindlessly walking. Before I knew it I ended up in front of an old apartment complex. The streets in this neighborhood were quiet, unlike the wreckage I had just left.

How long have I been walking? Where am I? Who is that woman staring at me?

Just as I realized where I was and who it was that was gazing at me, I collapsed.

"Honey, oh honey! Are you okay? What happened to you?" Ms. Smith was bending down next to me. She gently put her arm under my head and the other under my legs and carried me inside.

Oh, that peace again. What was it about Ms. Smith? Just being in her presence gives me comfort. Please save me. Oh...please just love me. I just want someone to love me.

Ms. Smith placed me gently down on the couch and walked in the kitchen. I could hear the clinking of glass and the running of water. She quickly came back and handed the glass of water to me. She again placed her arm gently under my head to help elevate it so I could drink.

"Sweetheart. What happened to you? You look so pale and thin." Ms. Smith took the empty glass from my hand and lifted my head enough for her to slip under and sit down. She placed a pillow on her lap and laid my head back down.

I just lay there quietly as Ms. Smith ran her fingers through my hair. She didn't urge me to talk; she just sat there quietly. All of the sudden she began to hum this sweet-sounding melody. I closed my eyes and drifted into a deep sleep. When I woke up, I could smell the sweet aroma of food. I heard the clanking of pots and heard Ms. Smith moving around in the kitchen. I sat up and made my way to where she was.

"I'm sorry I just showed up on your doorstep. I guess I was just walking mindlessly and ended up here," I said in a soft and low voice.

"It's okay, sweetheart. I am glad you came here. I have wanted to know how you are. After you left here, my heart wept for you. I have prayed for you every day," Ms. Smith shared.

"Ms. Smith, do you have any foster care children that are currently living here?" I asked. I am not sure why I wanted to know this, but for some reason I did.

"No honey. At this time I think it was God's plan for something else. I think He knew you would need the room."

Chapter Seven: Launch Pad to Healing

"Susan, honey, I am going to church this morning. Would you like to go with me?" Ms. Smith asked as she knocked on my bedroom door.

It had been about a week since the day I collapsed in front of Ms. Smith's place. She graciously agreed to allow me to stay with her with some stipulations. She shared that one of her expectations was that I would look for a job. Until I was working, she wouldn't charge me for any expenses. She did expect me to find work in the next three months, though. Ms. Smith explained that she didn't need my money; however, her wish was to help me learn to pay expenses and learn the skills I needed for responsible money management. I also needed to help around the house. I had a list of chores that I was responsible for each day.

"No, I am going to keep looking for work."

"All right, I hope you have a blessed day. I will be home around lunchtime. If you are back home by then, I would love for you to join me for lunch," Ms. Smith offered as she headed for the door. "Just remember, Susan. You are always welcome to come with me to church."

"I know, and thank you," I said with a forced smile on my face. "I just don't feel like I belong there."

"Well, let's talk about that more at lunch. You definitely belong there and everyone will love you. Just let me know when you are ready to go, and I will be right there beside you," said

Ms. Smith as she headed out the door.

I'm not good enough to go to church. The church would fall on me if I walked into it. With all the wrong choices I've made in my life, there is no way I could step into such a holy place. As soon as they found out I am pregnant and not married, they would kick me out anyway. Besides, maybe after I get myself cleaned up and my life in order, I can think about going to church.

I finished getting dressed and took a look in the mirror.

I am so ugly. I am starting to show. No one is ever going to marry me. I am not good-looking, and now I am pregnant. I should just go to the clinic and have this taken care of. I don't think I can do that, though. This is a child growing inside of me. But I don't have any way to support this child. I can't put it up for adoption. What if the family is like all the adults that have hurt me? I can't allow my child to go through that. What am I going to do?

I ran a brush through my hair and put it up in a ponytail. I didn't feel like bothering to make myself up today. I headed downstairs to the kitchen where I found a plate of eggs, pancakes, and bacon sitting on the table waiting for me.

I don't understand why Ms. Smith is so nice to me. What is it about her that is so different? Can she really care about me? No, she must get something out of doing this, but what?

I sat down and tried to eat the nice meal that Ms. Smith made for me, but I couldn't seem to get past the smell of it. Who would have thought that some little thing growing inside of you could make you feel so sick? I picked up my plate with the food that I barely touched and put it in the refrigerator. I spent the rest of the morning going around town and putting in job applications. I made it back home just in time to join Ms. Smith for lunch.

"How was your day?" Ms. Smith asked me as she placed a plate with a ham and cheese sandwich and some barbecue chips on it in front of me.

"It was okay. I went to apply for some jobs," I replied back.

"Susan, I wanted to talk to you some more about what you said before I went to church. Are you okay with that?" Ms. Smith asked as she sat down to join me at the table.

"I guess. I don't really remember what I said, though," I said as I picked up the sandwich and took a small bite out of it.

"Well, we were talking about you being welcome to come with me to church. I want you to know that no matter what choices you have made, no matter what you have done, that someone will always love and forgive you." Ms. Smith had finished this sentence and bowed her head over her food. After some time, she finally began to eat.

You are no good. Don't let her fool you. Don't be stupid. She is just playing you. She must want something.

"Ms. Smith, I really appreciate all that you are doing for me. However, church just isn't for me. I have made too many mistakes and messed up my life. God would never accept me. Maybe someday I can go to church, after I get my life in order," I said as I took another small bite of my sandwich. "Can I ask you a question?"

"Yes, of course you can ask a question. But Susan, honey, I told you to call me Rachel," Ms. Smith said. She had told me this for weeks, but I just had not gotten used to calling her by her first name.

"Would God be mad at me if I went to the clinic and ended the pregnancy? I mean, I just can't take care of a baby. I have no money…I am only nineteen years old. I would only make this child's life a mess like mine." I couldn't even look up at Rachel as the words came out of my mouth.

Rachel put her sandwich down and took a couple deep breaths.

Oh no, I made her mad at me. She is upset. She is going to hate me now that she knows what I want to do. Think…what can I say? How can I make this better?

I was ready for the yelling and who knows what else was to come, but that never came. Instead, Rachel just smiled at me and asked me what I thought.

"What do I think? I don't know. I guess that is why I am asking. I think He is going to hate me. I think He already hates me. I made such a mess…such a mess of my life." I couldn't hold back the tears any longer and began to cry. I pushed the plate away from me as I had lost my appetite.

"Well, I think that God would want you to think very carefully about the choices you have. I believe He is a loving God and that He loves the baby that is growing inside of you. I know that it is scary to think about everything it takes to care for a child. I want you to know that I am here for you and would be honored to help you through caring for this child." Rachel got up from her seat and came across to where I was and bent down and gave me a hug.

"I don't understand. Ms. Smith, I mean Rachel, why are you doing this? You are not being paid to care for me. I am not family. You have no reason to have even taken me in that day. Now you are saying you want to help me care for my child. I just don't understand any of this." My words could barely be heard through the sobbing.

Rachel pulled up a chair next to me. She looked me straight

in the eyes and pushed the lock of hair from my face to behind my ear.

"My dear, you really don't get it do you?" Rachel said. "I am sorry that so many people have hurt you. I know it's hard to trust that someone really does care about you and love you. There is no other reason other than I love and care about you. I do not need someone to pay me to love you. I do not need to receive something to love you. My love for you is a gift, and I expect nothing in return."

The tears continued to flow down my face. I couldn't believe that anyone would love me. To believe this meant possible heartache and pain. People have always left or hurt me. It's unsafe to open my heart to them.

"But why…why do you love me? I haven't done anything to deserve your love. I didn't treat you well when I was here. There is nothing special about me. I just don't understand it," I continued on, with my lack of understanding of what Ms. Smith was trying to express.

"Well, Susan, just like with God, I try to love people for who they are and who God created them to be. God created you as a masterpiece. Like when an artist finishes creating a beautiful painting, he stands back and looks at it and takes in its beauty. God created every part of you. He crafted you into the beautiful work of art that you are. He knows everything you did and everything you will become. He is with you all the time, and He wants you to come to Him with all that you are, all that you need and want to become. He, too, wants to give you a gift, the gift of salvation. He loves you and if you let Him, He will show you that He also forgives you for everything." Ms. Smith was so excited as she was sharing this with me.

There it is again. Something is different and peaceful about Ms. Smith. As she is sharing about God, her whole self radiates with joy. What is it about her? What is it about her God? How can I have this peace, this joy...whatever this thing is that Ms. Smith has?

NO, YOU CAN NEVER HAVE PEACE. YOU ARE STUPID. YOU ARE NOTHING LIKE MS. SMITH. YOU WILL NEVER BE HAPPY OR HAVE JOY. JUST GIVE UP!

I tried to push away these thoughts. Where were they coming from? Was I going crazy?

"Susan, are you okay?" Rachel asked with a concerned look on her face. "You seemed to have drifted off to somewhere else."

"I'm sorry. I was just thinking. I don't think I will ever be good enough for God to love me. I have done so many things wrong. I made so many mistakes. Why would he ever forgive or love me?" I tried to push back the tears as the words came out of my mouth.

"Oh, honey, God doesn't work that way. He is not some mean bully in the sky just waiting for us to make mistakes so that He can punish us. He loves us and knows what temptation is. He knows that we all make mistakes and fail, and He is ready to help us."

"Ms. Smith...I mean...Rachel, you just don't understand. God couldn't forgive me for going to the clinic and having them take care of the baby. He would hate me. Doesn't He say we shouldn't kill? Wouldn't that be killing? Would He forgive me if I gave the baby up for adoption? What if the family that takes the baby hurts it? What if I keep the baby and I hurt it? I don't know what I should do. I am so confused. How could I be so stupid? How could I let this happen to me?"

"Susan, the first thing you need to do is take a couple deep breaths. This is all a lot to take in and it is all very overwhelming. Let me tell you about my story. I believe it will help you understand better.

"When I was just a little bit younger than you, I got involved with a boy. His name was Tommy. Tommy was tall and handsome. He was everything a girl could want. However, Tommy had only one thing he wanted. I never wanted to sleep with him, but I was so afraid that he would leave me. I couldn't let that happen, so I gave in. Not long after we became intimately involved…well…I became pregnant. I didn't know what to do. I came from a very strict religious family. I couldn't tell them what had happened. So, I chose to end the pregnancy. Still to this day, I regret that choice."

"What happened between you and Tommy?"

"Well, Tommy didn't stick around long enough for me to tell him what choice I had made. As soon as he found out that I was pregnant he left and I never saw him again."

"Did you ever tell your parents what happened?"

"No, I didn't, and now it's too late. I live with my choices every day, but God has brought me healing from the situation. I know He has forgiven me. He forgave me long before I ever forgave myself. You see, Susan, I do know what you are going through. I believe that God knew that you would be going through this and He brought us together. He knew that when you first came here to my house that we would come to this very moment and be able to stand strong together."

"So then God let this happen to me?"

"No, honey, God lets us make our own choices. He tries to help us make the right decision. However, if we are not listening to Him or don't know He is there trying to help, we go our own way and can do things that lead to a difficult road."

"Thanks Ms. Smi…Rachel. I'm sorry, I am still getting used to not calling you Ms. Smith. I am really tired and think I am going to take a nap."

"Okay, darling. I am here if you want to talk more."

It was about five o'clock when the phone woke me up.

"Susan, it's for you. It's your sister, Amber," Rachel called to me from outside my bedroom door.

I had forgotten that I had even called her a couple of days ago. She was not home when I called, and I had left Rachel's number and asked for Amber to give me a call back. I ran down the stairs to the phone.

"Hello, Amber...how are you?" I asked with some sadness in my voice.

I knew that I hadn't reached out to Amber and Jonathan only but a handful of times since they removed us from my mom. My life had gotten so out of control. Part of me didn't want any responsibility for anyone besides myself; the other part of me didn't want my drama to impact Amber and Jonathan.

Chapter Eight: Family Crisis

I am not sure how long I had walked. The view from the bridge would have ordinarily been considered beautiful by most people; however, today the only thing I could think about was how far it was of a drop down. Would it kill me? Would it hurt?

The words echoed in my head: "...not that you have bothered to keep in touch with us."

Then I heard it again: YOU ARE WORTHLESS. NO ONE CARES ABOUT YOU. YOUR LIFE ISN'T WORTH ANY-THING. JUST END IT ALL.

I sat there staring at the water below for a long time, wondering what it would feel like to just free fall all the way to the rocks below. Then something strange happened, something I couldn't explain. I heard a still, small voice. "Susan. I love you. I care about you. I have plans for you."

Plans? What kind of plans? Plans to raise a baby on my own? Plans to live in misery the rest of my life? No, thank you.

"Susan, my love, my child. You are special, you are beautiful, and I have plans for you." There it was again. Where was that voice coming from? I looked around to see if there was someone close by whispering to me...nothing. The streets were empty and there was a stillness that surrounded me.

"Who is there?" I called out into the silent air. "Who are you and what do you want from me?"

"I want to give you a future—hopes and dreams. I will take care of you. Trust me."

Trust, what is trust? I can't trust anyone. Life is just full of pain and heartache. I can't keep going on like this. I need to just get out of here forever.

"Take my hand and let me take care of you. Give me your pains, your worries, and your fears, and I will give you dreams and hope and a future."

I wasn't sure what had just happened, but I had a sense of peace. I looked below at the rocks and the water and something told me that I couldn't do it. I took a few steps back from the ledge and climbed down to the pavement. I took a quick look around again to see if anyone had seen me, but there was no one around. What was the gentle voice that spoke to me? Was I going crazy?

I thought again of the words Amber had said to me. I had felt like I had let her down. I looked up at the sky and stared at the clouds as they passed overhead.

Why? Why did this all happen to us? Did we do something wrong? God, why do you hate us so much?

My cheeks could feel the warm liquid flowing out from my eyes: tears, something that seemed to come more often than before.

Did we offend you? Did we not pray enough? Is it because we never went to church? Why was I born? Why Lord, why? I just don't understand.

With my back up against the rails of the bridge, I sunk down into a fetal position and let the tears pour down my face. A car coming from the distance interrupted my thoughts. As the car came closer, I realized that it was Rachel's car. The car slowed down and stopped right in front of me. I tried to sink into the background so Ms. Smith wouldn't see me in my broken state, but it didn't help. Rachel stepped out of the car and was walking toward me. She sat down next to me and said nothing for a long time. It wasn't until I said something that she spoke.

"I'm sorry. I don't know what I'm doing anymore. I'm a mess." I couldn't even look up when I said the words. I felt so ashamed. So broken. The thought of seeing the anger and hurt in Ms. Smith's eyes was more than I could bear.

"Are you ready to go home?" Rachel said.

I suppose I never thought of Ms. Smith's—Rachel's—as home. But she called it that. Is that really home? Can it be that I belong somewhere?

"I need help, Rachel. I am afraid that I am going to hurt myself. I am afraid I am going to hurt the baby."

"Have you decided what you are going to do about the baby?" Rachel's tone was gentle and soothing.

"I guess I have. I don't know. I am not ready for being a mother. However, I can't give the baby up. There is something inside of me that says that ending the pregnancy is just wrong. So I feel like I don't have a choice; I have to keep the baby. I am just afraid."

"I think that you know in your heart what the answer is. It is completely understandable why you are afraid. But you are not in this alone." Rachel reached over and wrapped her arms around me. I hadn't felt safe in a long time, and for one split second I did. I felt all my worries and fears fall away.

***

We made it inside and found the telephone ringing. Rachel went over to answer the phone, and I felt the emptiness and loneliness beside me.

"Hello? Yes she is. May I ask who is calling? This is a friend

71

who she is staying with. Where is she? What is her condition?" I heard Rachel ask. My heart sank as I ran over to Rachel's side.

"Who is it? What happened? Is that for me?" Rachel held a finger up to signal me to wait a minute.

"Thank you, we will be there shortly." Rachel hung up the phone and the look on her face caused a heaviness in my chest, and all the muscles in my whole body tightened. "Honey, let's go into the living room and sit down." Rachel wrapped her arm around my shoulder and guided me in that direction.

"No, please tell me. Who was that on the phone? Is it about my sister and brother? Are they okay? Please just tell me!"

"Susan, your sister and brother are fine. It's your mother. She was in an accident. She is in the hospital. They said it's pretty serious. Put on your shoes and I will take you over there."

As much as I didn't want anything to do with my mother— she was the reason our family was broken apart—she was still my mother. I decided that I needed to make sure she was okay.

The car ride was painstakingly silent. I could feel the weight of every breath. It was only about a fifteen minute drive from the house to the hospital, but it felt like we had driven for hours. When we pulled up in front of the emergency room, I stopped breathing altogether. Rachel's voice jolted me back into reality, and I took in a deep breath as we entered the hospital.

***

"Hello, Susan. Mrs. Harris told me you called. What do you want?" Amber's voice sounded cold and distant.

"I wanted…I mean, I haven't…I wanted to talk to you. To see how you and Jonathan are doing. I know I haven't called in a while…" My voice trailed off and Amber interrupted me by cutting me off.

"We are fine, not that you have bothered to keep in touch with us. Susan, I really don't have time for this. Goodbye."

Before I had time to respond, I heard a dial tone.

SEE? YOU ARE WORTHLESS. YOU DIDN'T BOTHER TO WATCH OVER YOUR BROTHER AND SISTER. THEY DON'T CARE ABOUT YOU. YOUR LIFE ISN'T WORTH ANYTHING. YOU SHOULD JUST END IT ALL.

Chapter Nine: Helping the Helpless

"Mom, how could you let this happen to you? I can't hold the family together anymore. It was your responsibility to take care of us." I stood over my mother's broken body.

She had her arm in a cast, her face covered with bandages, and bruises from head to toe. Her skin was pale, and a machine was connected to her to help her to breathe. My mind couldn't process that this was really happening. I had to leave after shortly after entering the room.

When I got out into the hallway everything went black. When I opened my eyes again, I was looking up at the ceiling and there were a bunch of strange faces looking intently down at me.

"Honey, are you okay? You passed out," Rachel said.

"Just lay still, I am going to put your legs up on these blankets. Here take a sip of this, it's juice," a nurse said as she put a straw up to my lips.

I looked down at my feet only to have my gaze stop at my stomach. I could see my baby bump already. I feel like it was just yesterday that I found out I was pregnant. Panic came over me. With that came all the worries and fears flooding back.

What am I going to do? How am I going to care for this child? Look how much my parents messed us up, and now I am going to do the same to my child. I am not fit to be a mother.

I must have had a look of panic on my face, because the nurse's expression turned to concern. "Just breathe normally. Relax and take a few breaths."

"Can I sit up now?" I asked. I didn't want to continue to have the visual reminder of my condition. At least when I was standing I could forget about being pregnant if I didn't look down at my stomach.

"Just lay here a few more minutes. Here, take another sip of juice. Do you have any medical conditions?"

Rachel jumped in at that point and shared that I was pregnant and had not yet seen a doctor.

"I am fine, really. I just thought of how being a mother is overwhelming. I just need to sit up." The nurses helped me to sit up, but they all still had a look of concern on their faces.

"We should get you to a room and just make sure everything is okay," one of the nurses said.

"Really, I am okay. I was just overwhelmed." It didn't matter what I said; one of the nurses had already pulled a wheelchair over beside me and the two of them were helping me into it. It was no use fighting them. I could tell I wasn't going to win this battle. Besides, I was about four months along in my pregnancy now, and I still had not seen a doctor. Rachel tried day after day, week after week to get me to go see a doctor, but doing that required me to admit and recognize that I was pregnant. It was so much easier to live in denial if I just went about my life as I did before I was pregnant.

Up to this point, I still had not heard from Billy. About a month ago I had gotten up the courage to go back over to his apartment to try to talk to him; however, I found out at that time that he had moved. I didn't know where he had moved to and if he was even still living in the same city. I cried for days after this. How could Billy just leave me like that?

"Hold out your arm, we are going to take your blood pressure."

"Um, I don't have health insurance. I don't know how I am going to pay for this."

"Don't worry, sweetheart. We will have the social work department come down and talk to you and they will help you apply for insurance."

"No, thank you. I have had help from social workers before and trust me, it was not helpful."

My mind drifted back off to the day when the social worker came and took my siblings and me to separate foster homes. I remembered when my sister called with fear in her voice, begging for my help. I pleaded with the social worker to go help them, but they didn't do anything. And now, my sister and brother wanted nothing to do with me.

The nurses' chattering, the beeping machines, the screaming patients, the nurses poking at me, Rachel constantly watching over me…all prevented me from shutting the world out.

"I am going to put this solution on your stomach so we can take a look at the baby and make sure everything is okay. It might be a little cold, but it will not harm you or the baby."

The nurse spread a cold gel on my stomach. I kept my eyes tightly closed. I could feel my jaw clenching and the tears welling up in the corners of my eyes.

"Sweetheart, is there someone you want us to call?" one of the nurses asked me.

My mind went instantly to my mother's broken body just down the hall, and I quickly dismissed the thought.

"No, there's no one." The words slipped out of my mouth instinctively.

"Do you want to see the baby? She's beautiful."

"She?" I asked. "It's a girl?"

"Yes, it's a girl, and she looks healthy. She has a strong heart-beat and everything looks good."

Panic radiated through my whole body. I wanted to look, but at the same time I didn't. I slowly opened my eyes, keeping them focused on the ceiling, before I got the courage to look over at the monitor.

"How do you know it's a girl? How do you know everything is okay?" I asked as I looked at the black and white blob on the screen.

The nurses explained a bunch of medical things about how they are able to tell the baby is healthy and that it was a girl; however, I didn't hear much of what they were saying. Something inside of me was going on, a warmth of sorts.

Could this be joy? Was this happiness I really felt? So many things were a mess, that couldn't possibly be it. But what else could it be? I finally allowed my mind and feelings to connect, and it suddenly hit me…I was going to be a mother.

Chapter Ten: Preparing for the New Arrival

Two months had passed since my visit to my mother in the hospital. She was now home and recovering from her accident. I had been spending most of my time preparing for what was to come: Baby Abigail.

"Susan, how about this one?" Rachel asked as she pointed out a pink and white crib. "This one is adorable."

"Rachel, I can't afford this. It is way too expensive."

"Susan, we have been over this. I know that you do not want me to help and you want to pay for everything, but I am going to still buy the crib. Please do not worry about the cost."

With that, we purchased the crib. There was no point in arguing with Rachel. It was a battle I never seemed to win. We also purchased a car seat, a stroller, and many other baby items. I hated the thought of Rachel paying for all these things. I couldn't understand why she would do such a thing. I wasn't family, she didn't have any obligation, she wasn't court-ordered; she just did it.

It was Sunday morning and Rachel and I were heading to church. I had started going with her about a month ago. I didn't really understand everything they were talking about, but there was something that just gave me peace about going. My first time going I was afraid that everyone was going to judge me. They were not the way I expected at all; they were nice and they cared about me. They would ask me how the baby was doing and if they could pray for me. They genuinely seemed excited to see me. After church, Rachel took me out to lunch and then we did some more shopping.

"When we get home, I have a surprise for you, Susan," Rachel said on our drive home from the day's errands.

"Surprise? Rachel, you have given me so much. I don't deserve any of this. I still do not understand why you are helping me. You have bought the baby and me so many things and you have allowed me to stay at your home. I don't know how I am ever going to repay you."

"Some day, Susan, you will understand. For now, just know that I love you and that is why I am doing this."

When we got into the apartment I could smell fresh paint.

"Rachel, did you have someone here today painting?" I asked as I walked through the front hallway, past the kitchen.

"Come with me. We will go check it out together," Rachel said as she gently took my arm in hers and guided me toward the guest bedroom.

We approached the closed door to my bedroom. I could smell the paint even more strongly. Rachel instructed me to close my eyes, and with that, she guided me through the doorway into my room. When she told me to open my eyes, a shout of "surprise!" came from half a dozen church members. I looked around at my freshly painted room, decorated in pinks and purples. There were little teddy bear stickers on the walls and a little bear lamp on a table stand next to the pink and white crib that was filled with baby clothes and diapers. Next to the closet was also a changing table, filled with more diapers, baby wipes, and other baby items. I felt the constant flow of tears running down my face.

"I don't know what to say. I mean, I guess…I…well…why?" I couldn't quite figure out what to say. "Why did you all do this for me? I don't deserve it. You really do not know me. I am so overwhelmed."

"Susan, we love you. You are special. You deserve someone to love you and take care of you. You do deserve all of this and more. You do not need to earn it. We don't expect you to pay us back. We just want you to enjoy it and take care of the baby inside of you," said Tammy, one of Rachel's friends from church.

Everyone came up to me and gave me hugs and told me how special I was. I wasn't sure how I should respond. This was all so new to me. After the hugging fest ended, we all went into the living room and chatted for several hours. People took turns sharing about their past and their struggles.

Tammy shared about how she went from boyfriend to boyfriend until God finally got ahold of her heart and she changed how she lived her life. Molly shared that she grew up in a Christian home. However, when she went away to school, she stopped attending church. Molly shared that she just starting going again two years ago. Mark's story, though, was one that had the most impact on me.

"I grew up in a very hostile home. My parents fought all the time and my dad had no problem knocking my mom and us around." Mark pulled up his pant leg as he said this and revealed a scar that ran the length of his whole leg. "This is one of the results of my father knocking me around. My father is serving a life sentence in jail." There was a long silence after Mark said this. He took a deep breath and went on. "He was sentenced to life in prison after he killed my mom during one of his tirades." Tears started to flow down his cheeks. "I was there when it happened. It's a day I will never forget." Mark cleared the catch in his throat.

"It started with my father coming home from the bar. He had spent the night drinking with his buddies. My mom had been sick and was in bed all day. She didn't have the strength to get up to make dinner. My father was upset that there was no dinner cooked for him and went off on my mom. At first it was just yelling, but then my mom must have had enough of his yelling at her and she gave him a piece of her mind. That was all it took and my father flew across the room and wrapped his hands around my mom's neck." There was another long pause as Mark gathered himself.

"I…um…I tried to stop him, but it was no use. He was bigger and stronger than me. When I ran up to pull him away from my mother, he backhanded me so hard I flew against the room into the wall. I was temporarily knocked out. When…umm…when I came to, my mother was turning blue and gasping for air. My father's hands were wrapped so tightly around my mother's neck. I will never forget the look on my father's face…the look of pure anger and hatred in his eyes. There was nothing I could do. She died right before my eyes." Rachel had brought a box of tissues over to Mark and wrapped her arms around him. Everyone else in the room followed suit.

No words could have adequately filled the silence at that point.

Chapter Eleven: The Arrival

I was lying in bed, allowing Mark's story to run through my mind. I thought my parents were horrible people for what they did to our family, but what Mark's father did to his mother was so much worse. I tried to imagine what it would be like if I were in Mark's shoes. What would it have been like to watch my father kill my mother, right before my eyes, and there being nothing I could do about it. My stomach began to turn and I felt sick. I felt a sharp shooting pain in my stomach. At first I tried to ignore it, but it seemed to get worse. I got up a few times to go to the bathroom, but that didn't make the pain go away. As I was coming out from the bathroom on my last bathroom run, I felt something warm on my leg. I looked down and saw that I was standing in a puddle of what looked like water soaking my pajama pants.

"Rachel! Rachel! Please come help me!" I yelled as loudly as I could. I didn't care that it was only three o'clock in the morning. I didn't know what was happening to me and I needed someone. I needed Rachel. I needed my mom, but that was not an option.

"Honey, are you okay?" Rachel called to me as she stormed through my bedroom door. "Oh my, we need to get you to the hospital!"

"Rachel, I know you told me about the contractions and all the things I was going to go through, but I can't do this. I just can't do it."

"Susan, honey, you don't have a choice. I will be there with you. I think we should give your mom a call and let her know that you are in labor, though. Would that be okay? It's important to have our moms with us at times like this."

"She's probably not in any condition to drive. I don't want her to come and make a scene."

"Well, first things first. Let's get your overnight bag and get you to the hospital." Rachel grabbed my purple suitcase packed with all the things I would need after I delivered the baby.

What was I thinking? I can't do this? This thing, this baby...being delivered...by me! How am I supposed to take care of this little life? I can't even take care of myself.

I could feel my heart begin to race and my palms begin to get sweaty. I started to breathe like they taught me in the labor classes I went to, but it didn't seem to help. Everything was happening so quickly. One minute I was at home lying on my bed, the next I was in labor, and before I knew it, I was holding this little baby in my arms.

***

"I need to check your vitals," one of the nurses said as she held out her arms to take the baby from me. I didn't want to hand the baby over. There was a connection I had with her. After the nurse took my vitals, she gave me the baby back.

So tiny. Look at her fingers. What am I going to do with you? How am I going to take care of you?

"How are you doing?" Rachel asked, jerking me back into reality.

"What? Um, yes, I am fine. She is so beautiful and tiny. What do I do now?"

"Well, now you go be a mom," Ms. Smith said. "Speaking of moms, I think we should try calling your mom to let her know that Abigail was born. I am sure she would like it if you asked her if she would be a part of this."

"I guess, but I am afraid that she is going to come and be drunk. I don't want that for my child."

"Susan, I completely understand how you feel. How are you going to know if she is recovering if you do not give her a chance?"

"She has had her chances. Rachel, I want to forgive her, but because of her, my sister and my brother are in foster care. I was in foster care. Because of her, our lives are a mess. Why should I give her another chance?"

No sooner did the words come out of my mouth than I felt the regret of saying them. My mind went back to Mark's story about his mother and father, and my heart sank.

"I can see the hurt in your eyes, Susan. I know that what happened to you, what happened between your parents, and that your father leaving you has created so many scars on your heart. I pray that God allows your heart and scars healing."

Abigail started to cry, and a look of panic must have come over me because Rachel rushed to my side to show me how to gently rock the baby to sleep. I was thankful for the interruption, however not sure what to do to calm Abigail down. After the nurse came in to show me how to feed little Abigail, I was given time to get some sleep. I didn't really feel comfortable with them taking Abigail away and having her put in the nursery, but I was too tired to think about it.

"Susan...Susan. Please forgive me, Susan. Where are you? Susan, come back to me." I watched as my mother wandered around the woods aimlessly calling for me. As she continued

to roam through trees and over boulders, she gained more cuts and bruises. I watched as she stumbled over something and was about to fall straight down over a cliff.

Chapter Twelve: Soul Mending

My body jolted and I woke up. There were tears in the corners of my eyes. I could feel the fast-paced thumping in my chest. As I began to slow my breathing down to a normal pace, a vision shot across my mind of my mother tumbling around in the woods, lost. My mind continued to drift off again to Mark's story about his parents. I couldn't seem to shake the story from my head. Why should I forgive my mother? After all, she was the problem. She was the reason we were all in the mess we were in. But something inside me kept nagging at me.

Something that Rachel said to me a few weeks ago came back to mind: "Forgiveness is the start of healing." How could me forgiving my mother allow her healing from her drinking problem? I don't get it.

Oh Mother, why did you have to start drinking? Why did you have to push Amber? Why did Daddy have to leave us? I am unable to go to you at a time like this. You should be by my side to tell me what to do when Abigail is crying. Maybe if all of this didn't happen, I wouldn't have gotten pregnant. I wouldn't have had Abigail.

The very thought of that struck an aching chord in my heart. I wouldn't have had Abigail. Sweet little Abigail. My arms felt empty without her cradled in them. I rang for the nurse and had them bring Abigail back to my room. As I held her there in my arms and watched her sweet little innocent face, I felt my heart begin to melt. I suddenly wanted my mother to hold me. I reached over and grabbed the phone, quickly punching the numbers.

"Hello," was all that I managed to get out before a flood of tears began to stream down my face.

"Susan, Susan is that you?" the voice on the other end echoed back. "Susan, I miss you. I miss all of you so very much."

"Oh, Mom, I miss you too. I had the baby. I named her Abigail. She is beautiful. I want you to see her."

"You had the baby? Are you doing okay? Who is with you?" I could hear the sadness in my mother's voice. "When can I see her?"

"I want to make sure she is far away from the life that Amber, Jonathan and I have lived. I need to know that she is not going to see you drunk or the way we saw you. I want more for her. I need you to promise that to me."

There was a long pause before either one of us said anything. I could hear my mother's breathing on the other end, so I knew she was still there.

"Susan, I am sorry for everything that happened to you all. I wish I could go back and change the past, but there is no way. I want to make things right, now. I just need a chance. I know you are still angry at me, but please let me show you that I am different."

"I want to believe that. I really do. I just don't know how to start trusting again. I need a little more time. I will call you back when I am ready. I'm sorry, I have to go." I couldn't fight back the tears any longer. I hung up the phone and began to cry. I must have frightened Abigail, because she joined in crying with me. I rocked her how Rachel had shown me, and after what felt like forever, I got her to stop crying.

A WALK WITHIN

I was being discharged a couple days after Abigail was born. Rachel had arrived a couple of hours earlier to take Abigail and me home. I gathered all our belongings, and after we received the discharge paperwork, we finally left. As we left, I held this little wiggly thing in my hands. A baby…a mother…I'm a mother. A flash of panic came over me as we got to the car. I didn't know how to put the baby seat in the car. I didn't want Abigail to get injured if we got into an accident.

"Rachel, what do I do about the baby seat? I have no idea what to do. I didn't think of any of these little things." Tears ran down my face again. Why was I crying? What is wrong with me, I thought to myself.

"Susan, honey, I already took care of it. I installed the car seat before I came to pick you up. Let me show you what to do." Rachel took little Abigail from my arms and gently placed her in the car seat. She buckled her in and made sure everything was secure.

"Rachel, would you mind if I sat in the back? I want to watch over her and make sure she is okay." I didn't like that the baby would not be facing me. I wanted to make sure she didn't stop breathing or choke or something.

"That's okay, honey. Just know that you will not always be able to watch her. It's a scary thing being a new mom. To think that anything can happen when they are out of your sight. With time, you will get used to not having to watch over her twenty-four hours a day."

During the car ride home, I found myself glancing over at Abigail to make sure she was breathing. Every little noise that she made, every breath she took, made me jump.

"Does this ever get easier?" My voice broke through the silence in the car. I hadn't realized it, but Rachel was watching me from her rearview mirror.

"Yes it does, and no it doesn't. Parenting is always going to have its challenges, and you will always worry about her, but you will get used to the little things that seem so big," Rachel said as we pulled up to the apartment building.

We unloaded everything and headed inside. I glanced down again at Abigail as we were walking toward the building. She was content in her car seat. I gently rocked the seat back and forth as I walked.

YOU WILL NEVER BE A GOOD MOTHER! YOU WILL END UP JUST LIKE YOUR MOTHER. SHE'S GOING TO END UP IN FOSTER CARE JUST LIKE YOU DID.

There it was again: the discouraging thoughts. How could I stop it? Where was it coming from?

"Rachel, can we talk?" I asked after I put little Abigail down in her crib.

"Sure, honey. Let's go into the kitchen and I will make us some sandwiches."

Rachel headed for the refrigerator and grabbed the mayo, cheese, and sandwich meat. As she began making the sandwiches, I allowed the words to tumble around in my mind: *You will never be a good mother! She will end up in foster care…*

"Now what is it that you wanted to talk to me about?" Rachel asked as she placed a plate with a ham and cheese sandwich and chips on it in front of me.

"I know this is going to sound crazy. I guess I don't really know how to explain it."

"Go ahead. I will keep an open mind. I promise not to judge you," Rachel said as she took a bite out of her ham and cheese sandwich.

"Umm…well, have you ever heard…well, not heard, but

had thoughts that are just very discouraging? I mean, not like hearing voices, but thoughts that pop up in your head that make you...well, discouraged?" I knew I was fumbling through my words. I didn't want Rachel to think I was crazy.

"You are not crazy, honey. Your thoughts are powerful. They can cause you to become unmotivated and second guess...well, everything. It is important to have thoughts that are positive. To replace the negative, discouraging thoughts with positive ones."

"Positive thoughts. That's it. Rachel, now that sounds crazy. I can't just change my thoughts."

"Someday you will understand. For now, just know that you are not crazy," Rachel said as she came over and gave me a hug.

I was glad when she ended the conversation, because I was honestly growing tired of it. I heard Abigail stirring in her crib on the baby monitor. I had almost forgotten about her. I jumped up and quickly ran to the side of the crib. Was she breathing? Was she okay? Did she turn on her face? So many things to make sure that she was okay. This was harder than I thought. I stared down into Abigail's little face. I caressed her little fingers in my hand and thought to myself, *What do I do now?*

Chapter Thirteen: Family Reunification

It had been three months since little Abigail was born. I still had not allowed my mother to see her. Something inside me was afraid to open that door. My mother called every day, sometimes multiple times a day, to check in on the baby and me. How was I supposed to allow her back into my life? My brother and sister were still in foster care. I was trying to put the pieces together after my life fell apart.

I sat at the end of my bed, allowing the thoughts to stir in my mind: *She is the worst mother in the world. She messed up all our lives. She is such a failure. I can't stand her.*

As all the negative thoughts went through my mind, I remembered what Rachel had told me a while back. Just replace the negative thoughts with positive ones. I told Rachel that was crazy, but now what she told me came back to my mind. Positive thoughts. Well, why not?

My mother had had a hard life. She did mess up our lives, but maybe now she is better. She does call almost every day. What if I did allow her back into my life? No, it's too risky. This is stupid. Positive thoughts. Positive thoughts are not going to make my mother be a better person. Positive thoughts are not going to stop her from drinking or stop her from hurting us again.

My head hurt from the battle between good and bad thoughts.

I was tired of trying to fight the thoughts in my head. Why couldn't this be easier?

Forgiveness is the way to healing.

There it was again: one of the thoughts that just randomly popped up in my head. Good thoughts encouraging me, directing me. Not my thoughts, but whose? God's?

I put the thought out of my mind and went about my day. After I put Abigail to bed, I finally got myself ready for bed and laid there, just allowing the thoughts to roll through my mind.

Forgiveness. Forgive who? Forgive my father? Forgive my mother? Forgive all the foster parents that hurt me? Forgive God? Who am I supposed to forgive?

I heard it again: *Forgiveness is the way to healing.*

"WHO AM I SUPPOSED TO FORGIVE?" I shouted out loud.

Who was I talking to? I looked up at the ceiling and saw no one there. Is there really a God? Did He even hear me? If He does exist, He is probably busy taking care of more important people. Not someone like me who is a sinner.

"Forgiveness is the way to healing. I forgive you, and you, too, should forgive."

"God if that is you, tell me who I should forgive. Where do I start? How do I forgive?" I tasted the saltiness of the tears as they poured down my face. I was now on my knees beside my bed. "How? Tell me how!"

"Forgiveness starts with you."

I kneeled there at my bed for a long time, crying out to God. Exhausted, I eventually fell into a deep sleep.

In the morning I woke up to the birds chirping outside my window. I laid there for several minutes remembering the details of the strange encounter I had the night before, when it suddenly hit me: I need to forgive my mom. I need to forgive my father. I need to forgive my foster parents. But first I need to forgive myself. "Forgiveness starts with you." That is what the pastor had said. It starts with me forgiving myself first. Abigail's crying interrupted my thoughts. I rolled over and climbed out of bed and made my way over to her room.

As I cradled Abigail in my arms, I looked into her eyes. I'm so sorry, Abigail. I will be the best mother possible. I will care for you better than I was ever cared for. I will protect you. I will work on forgiving myself and forgiving those around me.

As I made my way down to the kitchen to make Abigail a bottle, I hummed her a soothing song. I wasn't quite sure why I was feeling so happy, but something inside of me seemed different.

"Oh, Abigail, I need to get my life together. Maybe I should go back to school. Wouldn't that be a good way to get my life back on track?"

"Yes, I think it is." Startled, I dropped Abigail's spoon on the floor. When I turned around I saw Rachel standing in the doorway.

"I didn't realize you were there. I was just talking out loud. I wasn't really serious," I said with a disappointing tone in my voice.

The clicking of Rachel's high heels across the tiles echoed in the silence. I felt the warmth of her hand rest on my arm. "I believe in you and I think you should go back to school."

"What about Abigail? There is no way I could leave her. Who would watch her?" The tone of sadness was unmistakable. I couldn't hide the emotions of my situation even if I had tried. I was a washed up teen and a high school dropout with a newborn.

I had quit my job after Abigail was born. I had to go on

public assistance to help cover my expenses. The reality was that I couldn't leave Abigail. I couldn't believe that just a few months ago I couldn't imagine what caring for a baby would have been like. Now I can't imagine what it would be like without Abigail. The very thought of her not being in my care and sight made me turn white.

"I will think about it," I halfheartedly told Rachel as I stood up and gave her an unconvincing hug. "I am going to the park with Abigail. I will be back later."

I just wanted the conversation to end. There was no way I could go back to school. I was a failure. I was a dropout. I was a mom. I cleaned all the green goo off from Abigail's chin and rubbed her little fingers with the damp cloth.

"How about we go for a walk? Yeah, that sounds good. Mommy can use some exercise." I felt the redness in my cheeks as I felt Rachel's stare upon me. I realized that I was speaking baby talk to Abigail.

"You know, you are really great with her." I looked over my shoulder at Rachel and saw the corners of her mouth stretching ear to ear. We both couldn't help but laugh.

"Thank you. I can't imagine doing this without you," I said to Rachel as I packed Abigail's things and strapped her into her stroller. I opened the door and my jaw dropped. There standing before me was my mother. "What are YOU doing here?!" I couldn't help my natural reaction of disbelief and anger.

"I know I should have called, but I knew that you wouldn't allow me to come over. There are some things I need to say, and I want you to hear me out. Can I come in?"

"No. Abigail and I were just leaving," I said in a loud and direct tone. Abigail began to cry almost immediately. "Now see what you did? You upset her."

"Please, Susan, can we talk? It is important." My mother

looked so much older than I remembered. She seemed different, but I still didn't trust her.

I unbuckled Abigail and cradled her in my arms.

"There, there. It's okay. The mean old woman was just leaving."

"Susan! That is your mother you are talking about." Rachel's voice came from behind me. "I know that you are upset, but you should still respect your mother."

"Fine. Come in. But you can't stay long. I will give you five minutes."

We all went into the living room and sat down on the couch. I rocked Abigail as she fell asleep in my arms. We sat and listened to her soft breaths.

"Susan. I know that words can never fix all the damage done. I know that I could never make up for the things your brother, sister, and you went through. I have worked on getting better. I went through a program to stop drinking. I am on the step for asking for forgiveness."

"Forgiveness. You are asking for forgiveness? Do you realize the damage done?!"

"Yes, Susan, I do. And unfortunately I cannot go back and fix it. I can only make things right going forward. I went back to court, and they agreed to allow your brother and sister to come back home and live with me," my mother said with shakiness in her voice.

I just sat in silence, stunned at what she had just said. How could a judge agree to put my siblings back into an unsafe situation, with her? Would my siblings be safe? How would I make sure they were safe? I had so many thoughts running through my mind. Abigail began crying again and jarred my attention back to reality.

"Why would the judge agree to do that?" I asked before thinking it through. "I mean, they are doing well where they are at." I tried to take the words back, but it was too late.

"Susan, I understand that this is hard, but they are my children. You are my child. Caring for them and caring for you is my responsibility."

"I can't do this. I need to get some air." I grabbed Abigail's stroller and dragged it behind me as I stormed out of the apartment.

By the time I got into the parking lot, I was out of breath. Abigail was crying again, and my mind was racing.

"ABIGAIL, STOP CRYING!" I shouted at her. She had a stunned look in her eyes. "Oh Abigail, I am so sorry! I didn't mean to yell at you," I said as I crumpled into a pile of mush in front of the apartment building.

How could I yell at her? She didn't do anything. I was just like my mother. I sat there crying with Abigail for several minutes before I got myself together and picked myself up off the ground.

"Come on, Abigail. Mommy will take you to the park now." I dried away the tears, buckled little Abby into her stroller, and headed off toward the park.

Chapter Fourteen: The Journey Ahead

I sat in the chair next to Rachel as the pastor preached a message on forgiveness. It seemed like I had heard this over and over again: forgiveness. I listened as he went on about how forgiveness sets us and the other person free. How unforgiveness is like drinking poison and expecting it to harm the other person. Something inside me was uncomfortable with what I was hearing. The pastor finished his message and I just sat there, allowing the words to soak in.

"I will go pick up Abigail from the nursery. You sit here as long as you need," I heard Rachel say.

"Thank you," I said. The words continued to tumble around in my head.

Deep down in my heart, I knew that I needed to make amends with my mother. I needed to rebuild a relationship with her.

After sitting for a short time, I gathered my belongings and headed to the lobby. I found Rachel and little Abby surrounded by several women.

"She is so adorable."

"Beautiful just like her mother."

"She is getting so big."

My heart smiled. They were saying such nice things about me and they didn't even know that I was there.

"How is she doing?" I asked as I approached the swarm of

women.

"She is doing great. She is getting so big," one of the women said.

Rachel and I collected Abby and all her things and headed out from the church. In the car, so many thoughts were floating around in my head, but I couldn't seem to get a handle on any of them. The tears started to run down my cheeks.

"What are you thinking about?" Rachel asked as we pulled up to the apartment complex.

I couldn't seem to find the words. The tears continued to flow.

"I don't know. I just can't help but think about what the pastor was saying. My heart is broken. I know that I have done things that God has seen as wrong, and I don't know that he will ever forgive me. I know that I need to forgive my mother, but I don't know how. There are so many thoughts I am having that it actually hurts to think. Does that make any sense?"

"Yes, honey, it does. Sometimes you have to take some time to allow the thoughts to sink into your heart a little at a time. The answers will come to you, you just need to keep seeking."

Rachel and I gathered Abby and headed into the apartment. As we approached the building, I saw a girl standing on the front steps. As we got closer, I could see that it was Amber. I hadn't seen my little sister Amber in a very long time.

"Amber, is everything okay? What are you doing here?" I asked with deep concern in my voice.

"Well, it's good to see you too," she retorted back.

"No, really, it's great to see you. You just have never come to visit me. Is everything okay? Are you okay? What happened?" I couldn't help but continue to question Amber.

"Everything is fine. I just needed to see you and talk some

things through," Amber said with sadness in her voice.

"Why don't you young ladies come on upstairs and I will make you some lunch," Rachel said as she opened the front door to the apartment building and summoned us to enter.

All of us piled into the small hallway and headed to Rachel's apartment. When we got into the apartment, I put Abby down for a nap and made my way back into the kitchen where Rachel was just putting down a few plates for lunch. As I sat down, Rachel scooped out some pasta from the pan on to our plates. She laid out some silverware and filled our glasses with milk.

"You ladies go ahead and talk. I am going to take my lunch in the other room and make some phone calls," Rachel said as she picked up her plate of food and headed into the other room.

"Amber, I really am glad to see you. I have missed you and Jonathan. I can't tell you how many times I picked up the phone to call but didn't have the words to say anything. I have so many regrets. I feel like a horrible sister."

"Susan, I know that we all had a difficult life. The situation that happened to us all was unfair. Susan, I came here because everything is not okay," Amber said with tears in her eyes.

"What do you mean?" I asked with worry in my voice.

"Well, Susan, I don't know how to say this, so I am just going to say it. Susan, I am pregnant."

My jaw dropped and we sat in silence. And so began a new journey in my life.

***

The words floated around the room in the stillness and silence. I couldn't believe what I just heard. My baby sister, only fifteen years old, was pregnant. It couldn't be. I must have heard her wrong.

"Wha....attt did you say?" were the only words I could get

out.

"Susan, I'm pregnant, and I am really afraid. I didn't mean for it to happen. I don't know what I am going to do. I didn't know who else to go to." Amber was crying uncontrollably now.

As soon as I came back to reality, I jumped up from my seat and ran over to her and wrapped my arms around her. We sat there embracing for a very long time.

"Susan, I don't have the strength like you do. I can't raise this baby. I want to go to the clinic and have them take care of it. I want you to go with me."

This is what the Lord says: I created you for a time such as this. I created you for a purpose.

Epilogue

Susan began her journey long before she ever knew it, facing heartaches and challenges throughout her life. Faced with her father abandoning her and the family at a young age, an alcoholic mother, foster care, peer pressure, sex, pregnancy, and much more, we see Susan overcome these obstacles.

Susan's mother continued to struggle with alcoholism her whole life. She fought to stay sober. She continued to attend support groups to help her stay on the right track. Determined to remain a part of her children's lives, she wanted to make up for the wrongs she had committed.

Amber and Jonathan returned home to their mother. Amber chose to keep the baby, and with the support of her sister, mother, and Rachel, she is raising a healthy baby boy.

Jonathan continues to struggle with finding his way. He has ended up in the wrong crowd—partying, drinking, and fighting against the wisdom his family tries to give to him. He is a victim of the wounds of his childhood. Maybe someday he will be able to heal from the cuts that life has dealt him, but for now, he continues going down the wrong path. His family, however, will never give up on him.

Susan returned to school and became a social worker. She began a career helping young girls who face similar challenges as she did, including pregnancy. Later in life she got married and had two more children. She attends church regularly, where she serves as a youth leader with her husband, and they are in the process of applying to become foster parents.

The End

Statistics

- 28% of U.S. students in grades 6–12 experienced bullying.[1]
- 20% of U.S. students in grades 9–12 experienced bullying.[1]
- 70.6% of young people say they have seen bullying in their schools.[1]
- 70.4% of school staff have seen bullying. 62% witnessed bullying two or more times in the last month and 41% witness bullying once a week or more.[1]
- 6% of students in grades 6–12 experienced cyberbullying.[1]
- 16% of high school students (grades 9–12) were electronically bullied in the past year.[1]

In one large study, about 49% of children in grades 4–12 reported being bullied by other students at school at least once during the past month, whereas 30.8% reported bullying others during that time.[1]

According to one large study, the following percentages of middle school students had experienced these various types of bullying:

Name calling (44.2 %); teasing (43.3 %); spreading rumors or lies (36.3%); pushing or shoving (32.4%); hitting, slapping, or kicking (29.2%); leaving out (28.5%); threatening (27.4%); stealing belongings (27.3%); sexual comments or gestures (23.7%); e-mail or blogging (9.9%) (cyberbullying occurs on cell phones and online)[1]

According to one large study, the following percentages of middle school students had experienced bullying in these various places at school:

Classroom (29.3%); hallway or lockers (29.0%); cafeteria (23.4%); gym or PE class (19.5%); bathroom (12.2%); playground or recess (6.2%)[1]

- Only about 20 to 30% of students who are bullied notify adults about the bullying.[1]

- Research indicates that persistent bullying can lead to or worsen feelings of isolation, rejection, exclusion, and despair, as well as depression and anxiety, which can contribute to suicidal behavior.[1]

- The vast majority of young people who are bullied do not become suicidal[1]

- Most young people who die by suicide have multiple risk factors.[1]

Laws

Currently there are no federal laws to help prevent bullying. There is legislation in 49 states regarding anti-bullying. However, bullying still is not illegal. If bullying becomes harassment, then it does break federal law.[1]

According to the CPS Involvement in Families with Social Fathers, there is a study that indicates that in many cases where the biological father is absent, there is an increased risk of child maltreatment.[2]

A study in the *Journal of Family Psychology* shows that being raised by a single mother increases the risk of teen pregnancy and marrying with less than a high school degree.[3]

The U.S. Census Bureau indicated that in homes where the father is absent, children are almost **four times** more likely to be poor.[4]

The U.S. Census Bureau indicates that **1 out of 3 or 24 million,** children in the United States, are living with absent biological fathers in the home.[5]

Safehorizon is an organization in New York, NY and is one of the largest victim services organizations in the United States. They have 57 program locations, ranging from shelters to legal services. Here are some statistics presented by the organization:

- **1 in 4** women will experience domestic violence during her lifetime.[6]

- Women ages **20 to 24** are at greatest risk of becoming victims of domestic violence.[6]

- Every year, more than **3 million** children witness domestic violence in their homes.[6]

- Children who live in homes where there is domestic violence also suffer abuse or neglect at high rates **(30% to 60%)**.[6]

- An estimated **1.3 million** women are victims of physical assault by an intimate partner each year.[7]

- **85%** of domestic violence victims are women.[7]

- Females who are **20-24 years of age** are at the greatest risk of nonfatal intimate partner violence.[7]

- Most cases of domestic violence are never reported to the police.[7]

- Over **25%** of abused children are under the age of three, while over **45%** of abused children are under the age of five.[8]

- **In 2012 there were 1,593** children in the United States who died because of abuse or neglect.[8]

- Every year there are approximately **2.9 million** reports of child abuse in the United States.[8]

- **25% of abused children are** more likely to experience teen pregnancy.[8]

- **According to one study, 80%** of children met criteria for at least one psychiatric disorder by age 21, including depression, anxiety, eating disorders, and suicide attempts.[8]

Sources

[1] http://www.stopbullying.gov/news/media/facts/

[2] "CPS Involvement in Families with Social Fathers." Fragile Families Research Brief No. 46. Princeton, NJ and New York, NY: Bendheim-Thomas Center for Research on Child Wellbeing and Social Indicators Survey Center, 2010.

[3] Teachman, Jay D. "The Childhood Living Arrangements of Children and the Characteristics of Their Marriages." Journal of Family Issues 25 (January 2004): 86-111.

[4] U.S. Census Bureau, Children's Living Arrangements and Characteristics: March 2011, Table C8. Washington, D.C.: 2011.

[5] Howard, K. S., Burke Lefever, J. E., Borkowski, J.G., & Whitman, T. L. (2006). "Fathers' influence in the lives of children with adolescent mothers." Journal of Family Psychology, 20, 468- 476.

[6] http://www.safehorizon.org/page/domestic-violence-statistics--facts-52.html

[7] National Coalition Against Domestic Violence, Fact Sheets, http://www.ncadv.org/files/DomesticViolenceFactSheet(National).pdf

[8] http://www.safehorizon.org/page/child-abuse-facts-56.html

Resources

If you are in danger, please use a safe computer, or call 911, your local hotline, or the U.S. National Domestic Violence Hotline at 1-800-799-7233 and TTY 1-800-787-3224.

Dating/Relationship:

http://www.loveisrespect.org/
Provides resources for teens, parents, friends and family. Communication is confidential and anonymous.

http://www.domesticviolence.org
A resource that provides a handbook about domestic violence as well as valuable resources. You will find information that will help you or those you care about get support and make a safety plan.

http://chooserespect.engagethecrowd.com/
This is a resource that is an initiative to help teens form healthy relationships and prevent dating violence before it ever starts. It is a valuable resource for parents, caregivers, older teens, educational providers, or anyone else that desires to motivate teenagers to become proactive in learning about dating violence and in forming respectful and healthy relationships.

http://www.loveisnotabuse.com
Provides tools that anyone can use to learn about the issue and to find out how they can help with the epidemic of domestic violence.

http://www.startstrongteens.org
This is a resource that provides support with anyone working with teens on dating violence prevention.

http://www.thatsnotcool.com
This is a resource developed by the Family Violence Prevention Fund designed to help prevent teen dating abuse. This site uses digital examples to help teens draw their own conclusions about what is, or is not, acceptable relationship behavior.

Suicide Resources:

The Jason Foundation, Inc.
http://jasonfoundation.com/
The Jason Foundation provides information, education programs, and resources to help in the fight against the "silent epidemic" of youth suicide.

The Suicide Prevention Action Network USA
http://www.afsp.org/advocacy-public-policy/become-an-advocate
A suicide prevention organization dedicated to generate grassroots support among suicide survivors.

American Association of Suicidology
http://www.suicidology.org/home
AAS is a membership organization for all those involved in suicide prevention and intervention, or touched by suicide. Its website includes resources for helping those who are struggling with depression and suicidal thoughts, and inspirational stories from suicide attempt survivors.

Emotions & Depression

Teen Moods
http://www.teen-moods.net/

Teen Moods is a depression support community created by an adolescent with depression, and is open to all including teens and parents.

Depression Forums
http://www.depressionforums.org/
A supportive, informative website that offers a caring, safe environment for members to talk to their peers about depression, anxiety, mood disorders, medications, therapy and recovery.

Families for Depression Awareness
http://www.familyaware.org/
An organization that helps families recognize and cope with depressive disorders, and prevent suicide. Its website contains helpful resources and inspirational stories about recovering from mental illness.

DepressedTeens
http://www.thebalancedmind.org/flipswitch/podcast
This website provides valuable information/educational resources for teenagers, their parents and educators to understand the signs and symptoms of teenage depression and get help when needed.

Alcohol-related Resources:

24-Hour Addiction Helpline
(888) 828-2502

Al-Anon: A resource for family members of alcoholics.
http://al-anon.alateen.org/

Designation Hope: A women's addiction & mental health treatment center
http://alcoholtreatmentcenter.org/

Teen Challenge USA: Helps adults and teens to find freedom

from addiction
(417) 581-2181
http://teenchallengeusa.com/

Alcoholics Anonymous: Self-supporting, nonprofessional group for individuals seeking freedom from a drinking problem
http://www.aa.org/

Hotlines:

National Teen Dating Abuse Helpline: 1-866-331-9474, or TTY 1-866-331-8453

National Suicide Hotline: 1-800-SUICIDE (784-2433)

National Suicide Prevention Lifeline: 1-800-273-TALK (8255)
Both toll-free, 24-hour, confidential hotlines which connect you to a trained counselor at the nearest suicide crisis center.

Safe Place: 1-888-290-7233
Project Safe Place provides access to immediate help and supportive resources for young people in crisis through a network of qualified agencies, businesses, and trained volunteers in 32 states.

National Alliance of the Mentally Ill: 1-800-950-6264
Toll-free, confidential hotline operating Monday through Friday, 10 a.m.- 6 p.m. (EST). Trained volunteers provide information, referrals, and support to anyone with questions about mental illness.

CPSIA information can be obtained at www.ICGtesting.com
Printed in the USA
BVOW11s1343040815

411250BV00005B/18/P